THE BEGINNER'S BLUEPRINT TO INTERMITTENT FASTING

Simple Science, Practical Plans, and Real Results

Dr. Rebecca Ellington

Copyright © 2025 Dr. Rebecca Ellington

All rights reserved.
No part of this book may be reproduced, distributed, or transmitted in any form or by any means, including photocopying, recording, or other electronic or mechanical methods, without the prior written permission of the author, except in the case of brief quotations embodied in critical reviews and certain other non-commercial uses permitted by copyright law.

Disclaimer:
The information contained in this book is for educational and informational purposes only. It is not intended as medical, health, or professional advice. The author is not a medical professional, and the content should not be used as a substitute for professional guidance. Always consult a qualified healthcare provider or expert before making any significant changes to your diet, lifestyle, or health practices. The author and publisher disclaim any liability for any adverse effects resulting from the use or application of the information contained in this book.

Publisher's Note:
This book is independently published by the author. The author has taken great care to ensure the accuracy and completeness of the information provided. However, the author and publisher assume no responsibility for errors, inaccuracies, omissions, or any inconsistency herein.

Trademarks:
All trademarks, service marks, and trade names mentioned in this book are the property of their respective owners. The use of any trademark in this book does not imply any affiliation with or endorsement by the trademark owner.

Attributions:
The author has made every effort to provide proper attribution for any third-party content, including quotes, studies, and references. If any attribution is missing or incorrect, please contact the author for correction in future editions.

CONTENTS

Title Page

Copyright

Introduction: Your First Step: Why Fasting Changes Everything — 1

Chapter 1: The Basics That Change Everything — 10

Chapter 2: Your First Fasting Journey: Getting Started and Choosing Your Path — 30

Chapter 3: Food, Drink, and the Science of Your Body — 56

Chapter 4: Overcoming Challenges and Making Fasting Your Own — 82

Chapter 5: Special Considerations: Women's Health, Activity, and Exercise — 111

Chapter 6: The Inner Experience: Mental Clarity, Emotional Growth, and Tracking Progress — 137

Chapter 7: Finding Meaning: Cultural Traditions and Deepening Your Practice — 161

Chapter 8: Staying Safe and Finding Support — 183

Chapter 9: Success Stories: Real Beginners, Real Results — 207

Chapter 10: Your Complete 30-Day Beginner's Plan	236
Chapter 11: Beyond the Basics: Questions, Answers, and Moving Forward	272
References and Bibliography	328

INTRODUCTION: YOUR FIRST STEP: WHY FASTING CHANGES EVERYTHING

I remember the moment Sarah realized something profound had changed. It wasn't when her clothes began fitting differently, though that had certainly happened. It wasn't even when her doctor expressed pleasant surprise at her improved bloodwork. The moment came on an ordinary Tuesday afternoon as she sat at her desk, three hours past lunch, working on a challenging project. She suddenly became aware that she was completely focused, mentally sharp, and—most surprisingly—not thinking about food at all.

"For the first time in my adult life," she told me later, "I wasn't watching the clock waiting for my next meal. I wasn't anxious about hunger. I was just... present. Engaged with my work. That's when I knew this wasn't just another diet I was trying. Something fundamental had shifted in my relationship with food and with my body."

Sarah had discovered what you're about to learn: intermittent fasting offers something far more valuable than just another weight loss strategy. It provides a pathway back to your body's natural rhythms—a return to an eating pattern that humans evolved with for thousands of years before our modern world of 24/7 food availability.

As you begin this journey, you might be carrying the weight of previous disappointments. Perhaps you've tried countless diets that started with enthusiasm and ended in frustration. You may have experienced the initial success followed by the disheartening plateau, or worse, the rebound weight gain that left you feeling defeated. Those experiences can create layers of doubt, self-criticism, and scepticism that make it difficult to approach any new health practice with genuine hope.

I want to acknowledge those feelings right now. They're valid. They're common. And they're based on very real experiences that deserve respect.

But I also want to offer a perspective shift that many have found liberating: intermittent fasting is fundamentally different from dieting. Instead of adding another set of complicated rules about what you can and cannot eat, fasting simply creates a framework for when you eat. Instead of fighting against your body's natural processes, it works with them. Instead of creating a sense of deprivation, it cultivates a sense of natural rhythm and, eventually, freedom.

How This Book Is Different

You may have noticed there's no shortage of books about intermittent fasting on the market. So why add another? Because in my years of guiding people through this process, I've consistently observed a gap between the deeply technical science-focused books and the oversimplified "quick-fix" approaches. What's been missing is an accessible guide specifically designed for true beginners—one that respects both your intelligence and your need for straightforward guidance.

This book differs from others in several important ways:

First, it maintains a deliberate beginner-appropriate pace. We won't dive into advanced fasting protocols in the early chapters, nor will I assume you have prior knowledge of metabolic processes or nutritional science. We'll build your understanding systematically, introducing concepts when you're ready for them.

Second, this book strikes a careful balance between scientific rigor and everyday accessibility. You'll gain a solid understanding of the physiological processes that make intermittent fasting so effective, but explained through relatable metaphors and clear language rather than technical jargon.

Third, we focus on sustainable lifestyle integration rather than quick-fix results. While many resources emphasize rapid transformation, this book prioritizes changes you can maintain for years to come. The goal isn't a dramatic six-week makeover but rather a comfortable, adaptable practice that becomes as natural as brushing your teeth.

Fourth, throughout these pages, you'll find special attention to the emotional and psychological aspects of changing eating patterns. Food is deeply personal and emotionally charged for most of us. Acknowledging and working with these emotional dimensions is essential for lasting success.

Fifth, you'll follow a clearly structured progression that takes you from complete novice to confident practitioner. Each chapter builds on the previous one, creating a supportive scaffold for your learning and implementation.

Sixth, you'll find practical application tools embedded throughout the text that promote immediate implementation. These "Try This Now" experiments, "Decision Point" frameworks, and "Implementation Checklists" transform abstract concepts into concrete actions you can take immediately.

Seventh, visual learning strategies make complex concepts accessible. From timelines showing what happens in your body during fasting to decision trees helping you select the right approach for your lifestyle, these visual elements support different learning styles and enhance comprehension.

Finally, you'll receive responsible, nuanced guidance about safety and personalization. Rather than offering one-size-fits-all prescriptions, this book acknowledges the beautiful uniqueness of your body and circumstances, providing frameworks for adapting fasting to your specific needs.

How to Use This Book

Different readers approach books in different ways, and this resource is designed to support various learning styles and needs. If you prefer a comprehensive understanding before taking action, you might want to read the entire book from beginning to end before implementing your fasting practice. The chapters build upon each other, providing a progressive journey from basic concepts to practical application.

However, if you're eager to get started right away, you might prefer to read this introduction and Chapter 1 for foundational understanding, then jump ahead to Chapter 10: Your Complete 30-Day Beginner's Plan to begin implementation. You can then return to the intervening chapters as questions or challenges arise.

If you have specific concerns or circumstances, the "Start Here If..." section below will guide you to the most relevant initial chapters for your situation.

Throughout the book, you'll find interactive elements designed to engage you directly with the material:

1. "Try This Now" micro-experiments invite you to experience concepts firsthand
2. Journaling prompts help you reflect on personal insights
3. Self-assessment tools track your progress beyond the scale
4. "Pause and Consider" moments encourage deeper engagement with challenging concepts
5. "Decision Point" frameworks help you make personalized choices

I encourage you to engage with these elements rather than skipping over them. They transform passive reading into active learning and personal discovery.

Important Health Disclaimer

Before we go further, I must emphasize that this book

is intended as educational information, not medical advice. The information provided here is based on scientific research and practical experience, but it cannot replace the personalized guidance of healthcare professionals who know your specific medical history and needs.

Intermittent fasting is not appropriate for everyone. If you have any existing medical conditions—particularly diabetes, history of eating disorders, pregnancy or breastfeeding status, or are taking medications that require food—please consult with your healthcare provider before beginning any fasting practice. Children, adolescents, and elderly individuals with health concerns should also seek medical guidance before implementing intermittent fasting.

Even if you're generally healthy, I strongly recommend discussing your interest in intermittent fasting with your healthcare provider. They can help monitor your response and make appropriate adjustments to any medications or treatment plans.

Throughout this book, I'll highlight specific considerations and cautions, but these should complement, not replace, personalized medical advice.

Start Here If...

While the book is designed for sequential reading, your specific circumstances might make certain chapters particularly relevant as starting points:

If you have a demanding physical job or athletic training schedule: Begin with Chapters 1 and 5 to understand how to adapt fasting to high energy demands.

If you have previous dieting trauma or a complicated relationship with food: Chapters 1, 6, and 8 provide foundations for approaching fasting with emotional intelligence and proper support.

If you're managing a health condition with your doctor's approval: Chapters 1 and 8 offer guidance on safety considerations and working with healthcare providers.

If you're a woman concerned about hormonal impacts: Chapters 1 and 5 address women's specific considerations with fasting.

If you're struggling with emotional eating: Chapters 3 and 6 explore how fasting can help transform food relationships and emotional patterns.

If you're looking for deeper meaning beyond physical benefits: Chapters 1 and 7 connect fasting to cultural traditions and deeper personal growth.

If you need support or accountability: Chapter 8 provides guidance on building effective support systems and finding community.

Beginning Your Journey

As we conclude this introduction, I'd like to invite you to approach this journey with a spirit of curiosity and self-compassion. The path ahead isn't about rigid rules or deprivation—it's about rediscovering your body's innate wisdom and capacity for balance.

You're about to embark on a process of self-discovery

that extends far beyond changing when you eat. Many people find that intermittent fasting becomes a doorway to greater body awareness, emotional intelligence around food, and a sense of empowerment that spreads into other areas of their lives.

There will be adjustment periods and challenges along the way—that's part of any meaningful change. But there will also be moments of genuine revelation, when you realize your relationship with food, hunger, and your own body has transformed in ways you hadn't imagined possible. Like Sarah's Tuesday afternoon epiphany, these moments often arrive quietly, in the midst of ordinary life, when you suddenly recognize that something fundamental has shifted.

In the chapters ahead, we'll walk through everything you need to know—from the fascinating science behind why fasting works to practical day-by-day guidance for your first month. We'll explore how to adapt fasting to your unique body, lifestyle, and goals. We'll address challenges directly and celebrate victories meaningfully.

This isn't just another diet book. It's an invitation to reclaim your natural relationship with food, hunger, and satisfaction. It's a pathway to understanding your body's remarkable adaptive capabilities. And for many, it becomes a surprising source of freedom in a world where constant consumption is often the default.

Turn the page when you're ready to begin. Your body already knows how to fast—it's been waiting for you to rediscover this natural rhythm. I'm honoured to guide you through the process of making intermittent fasting a comfortable, sustainable, and transformative part of your life.

CHAPTER 1: THE BASICS THAT CHANGE EVERYTHING

What You'll Discover

By the time you finish this chapter, you'll have a clear understanding of what intermittent fasting actually is (and isn't), the fundamental science behind why it works, and how it differs from conventional diets you may have tried before. You'll learn about the surprising range of benefits that extend far beyond weight management, gain insight into what happens in your body during different fasting durations, and discover tools to address the most common concerns that beginners face. Most importantly, you'll begin developing the mindset that transforms intermittent fasting from a temporary diet into a sustainable practice that works with your body's natural rhythms rather than against them.

One Person's Transformation

When Michael first considered intermittent fasting, weight loss wasn't actually his primary goal. At 42, he carried about fifteen extra pounds he wouldn't have minded losing, but what really concerned him was his fluctuating energy levels. By mid-afternoon each day, his mental focus would evaporate. He'd find himself staring at his computer screen, unable to concentrate, often reaching for another coffee or a snack to power through. Despite eating what he considered a healthy diet—whole grains for breakfast, a decent lunch, healthy snacks—he experienced constant energy crashes that affected his work performance and left him feeling depleted by evening.

"I was eating all the 'right' foods," Michael explained, "but I was eating all day long because I thought that's what kept my metabolism running. The irony is I felt hungry almost constantly, even though I was never going more than a few hours without food."

Michael's experience is something I'll reference throughout this chapter because it illustrates something profound about fasting that surprises many beginners: the benefits often extend far beyond what you initially seek. While Michael was hoping to stabilize his energy, he discovered improvements in areas of his life he hadn't even considered might be connected to his eating patterns.

Let's explore the science that explains why Michael—and so many others—experience such comprehensive changes when they adopt intermittent fasting.

The Science Behind Intermittent Fasting

The research supporting intermittent fasting has exploded in recent years, with studies coming from prestigious institutions worldwide. Rather than overwhelming you with technical details, I want to highlight the most compelling findings and introduce you to a few pioneering researchers whose work has advanced our understanding.

Dr. Valter Longo, director of the Longevity Institute at the University of Southern California, has conducted groundbreaking research on fasting and longevity. His work shows how fasting periods trigger cellular "cleanup" mechanisms that may contribute to longer, healthier lives. His studies have demonstrated that fasting promotes the process of autophagy—essentially your cells' self-cleaning system—which removes damaged components and refreshes cellular function.

Dr. Satchin Panda at the Salk Institute has pioneered research on circadian rhythms and time-restricted eating. His studies reveal that aligning our eating patterns with our body's internal clock optimizes metabolic health. This research explains why simply changing when you eat, without necessarily changing what you eat, can produce significant health improvements.

Dr. Mark Mattson, formerly of the National Institute on Aging and now at Johns Hopkins University, has extensively studied fasting's effects on brain health. His research indicates that the mild stress of fasting actually strengthens neural connections and may protect against neurodegenerative diseases.

What's particularly striking about this research is the consistency of findings across different populations and fasting methods. From improved insulin sensitivity to reduced inflammation, the benefits appear regardless of whether the fasting protocol is daily time-restricted eating or alternate-day approaches.

For Michael, this science translated into real-life improvements: "After about two weeks of practicing 16:8 fasting [16 hours fasting, 8 hours eating], I noticed I could work straight through the afternoon without that brain fog I'd been fighting for years. It was like someone had cleared the static from my mental radio signal."

What Exactly Is Intermittent Fasting?

At its simplest, intermittent fasting is a pattern of eating that alternates periods of voluntary abstinence from food with periods of regular eating. Unlike traditional diets that focus on what you eat, intermittent fasting primarily addresses when you eat.

Think of intermittent fasting as working with your body's natural ebb and flow rather than imposing artificial restrictions. It's less like forcing your body into an unnatural state and more like synchronizing with rhythms that have been part of human physiology throughout our evolution.

A helpful analogy is to imagine your body as a dual-engine vehicle. One engine burns food for fuel (especially carbohydrates), while the other burns stored fat. The problem in modern life is that most people never give the second engine—the fat-burning one—a chance to fully activate because they're constantly providing new fuel through frequent eating. Intermittent fasting simply creates the conditions that allow your body to switch from one engine to the other.

Common intermittent fasting approaches include:

Time-Restricted Eating (TRE): Concentrating your daily food intake within a specific window, such as 8 hours, and fasting for the remaining 16 hours (often written as 16:8). This is what Michael adopted.

Modified Alternate-Day Fasting: Alternating between days of normal eating and days of significant calorie reduction (typically consuming about 500-600 calories on "fasting" days).

5:2 Method: Eating normally five days per week and significantly reducing calories on two non-consecutive days.

24-Hour Fasts: Completing a full 24-hour fast once or twice per week.

What intermittent fasting is NOT is equally important. It's not about severe calorie restriction across all days. It's not about eliminating food groups. It's not about obsessing over specific macronutrient ratios. And critically, it's not about ignoring your body's signals—rather, it's about rediscovering how to interpret those signals accurately.

Our Fasting Heritage: Not a Trend but a Return

Although intermittent fasting may seem like a modern health trend, it actually represents a return to eating patterns that shaped human evolution for millennia. For most of human history, constant access to food was the exception, not the norm. Our ancestors experienced natural periods of feast and famine, and our bodies evolved sophisticated mechanisms to thrive under these conditions.

From an evolutionary perspective, our ability to function—in fact, to function optimally—during periods without food was essential for survival. If hunger immediately produced debilitating weakness, our species would have perished long ago. Instead, many of the metabolic pathways activated during fasting actually enhance physical and mental performance, likely as an adaptation that helped our ancestors successfully hunt and gather food.

Beyond evolution, fasting has deep cultural and spiritual roots across human civilizations. From the ritual fasts in virtually all major world religions to the therapeutic fasts prescribed by Hippocrates, the "father of medicine," humans have recognized fasting's transformative potential for thousands of years. Traditional medicine systems worldwide—from Ayurveda to Traditional Chinese Medicine—incorporate fasting as a healing practice.

When you begin intermittent fasting, you're not adopting a contemporary fad; you're reconnecting with a fundamental human rhythm. The truly modern eating pattern isn't fasting—it's our current habit of constant consumption, grazing from morning until night, which has only become normal in the last few generations.

Michael found this perspective shift profoundly meaningful: "Realizing that fasting is actually the more natural human pattern while constant eating is the modern anomaly changed how I thought about hunger. Instead of seeing hunger as an emergency, I began to recognize it as a normal, natural sensation that doesn't need immediate resolution."

The Benefits: Beyond Weight Management

While many people initially come to intermittent fasting for weight management, the range of potential benefits extends far beyond the scale. Let's explore the most well-supported advantages:

Metabolic Flexibility: Perhaps the most fundamental benefit is developing metabolic flexibility—your body's ability to efficiently switch between using carbohydrates and fat for fuel. This flexibility contributes to stable energy levels throughout the day, reducing the crashes and cravings many people experience. For Michael, this was the game-changing benefit: "I used to be at the mercy of my blood sugar. Now I can go hours without eating and maintain steady energy and focus."

Improved Insulin Sensitivity: Regular fasting periods can increase your cells' responsiveness to insulin, the hormone that regulates blood sugar. Better insulin sensitivity is associated with reduced risk of type 2 diabetes and improved management of existing diabetes (though diabetic individuals should only fast under medical supervision).

Cellular Renewal Through Autophagy: Fasting activates autophagy, your body's process of cleaning out damaged cells and generating new ones. Think of it as your cellular "housekeeping" system, which may contribute to longevity and reduced disease risk.

Enhanced Brain Function: Many practitioners report improved mental clarity, focus, and cognitive function during fasted states. Research suggests this may result from the production of brain-derived neurotrophic factor (BDNF), which supports neural health and new connection formation.

Reduced Inflammation: Chronic inflammation underlies many modern diseases. Studies indicate that various fasting protocols can reduce inflammatory markers in the body, potentially offering protection against inflammatory conditions.

Cardiovascular Benefits: Research shows improvements in heart disease risk factors, including blood pressure, cholesterol profiles, and triglyceride levels for many who practice intermittent fasting.

Simplified Relationship with Food: Beyond physical benefits, many people report psychological benefits—freedom from constant thoughts about food, reduced emotional eating patterns, and a more mindful approach to nutrition.

Digestive Rest and Repair: Fasting provides a break for your digestive system, which rarely gets downtime in conventional eating patterns. Many report improved digestive comfort and reduced symptoms like bloating or reflux.

For Michael, these benefits compounded over time: "The mental clarity came first, within about two weeks. The steady energy followed shortly after. Then I noticed my sleep improving—I used to wake up several times a night, but after a month of fasting, I was sleeping straight through. Weight loss happened gradually without me focusing on it—about 15 pounds over three months. The most surprising benefit was how my seasonal allergies became much less severe. I never would have connected that to my eating pattern."

Separating Fact from Fiction

As intermittent fasting has grown in popularity, so too have misconceptions about how it works and what it does. Let's address some common myths with evidence-based corrections:

Myth: Fasting puts your body into "starvation mode," slowing metabolism. Reality: Short-term fasting (the kind practiced in intermittent fasting) does not slow metabolism. In fact, some studies show temporary increases in metabolic rate during fasting periods due to the release of norepinephrine, which helps mobilize fat stores. True metabolic slowing typically occurs only with prolonged caloric restriction lasting many days or weeks—not the intermittent patterns we're discussing.

Myth: You must eat every 2-3 hours to "stoke your metabolism." Reality: There's no scientific evidence that frequent eating increases metabolic rate. The thermic effect of food (calories burned during digestion) depends on the total amount of food consumed, not how often you eat it.

Myth: Fasting causes muscle loss. Reality: While extremely prolonged fasting could eventually impact muscle tissue, the short fasting periods in intermittent fasting do not lead to significant muscle loss, especially when combined with adequate protein intake during eating windows and regular resistance exercise. In fact, the increase in growth hormone during fasting may actually help preserve muscle.

Myth: Breakfast is the most important meal of the day; skipping it destroys health. Reality: The famous adage about breakfast originated largely from cereal company marketing, not scientific evidence. While some individuals genuinely feel best with breakfast, many thrive when extending their overnight fast through morning hours. The best approach depends on your body's unique response and your lifestyle needs.

Myth: Fasting causes your body to "eat your muscles" before burning fat. Reality: Your body has evolved sophisticated mechanisms to preserve muscle tissue during food scarcity. During short-term fasting (up to 24-36 hours), your body primarily burns stored glycogen and fat while preserving muscle tissue through various metabolic adaptations.

Myth: Fasting will tank your energy and make exercise impossible. Reality: After an adaptation period, many people report enhanced energy and workout performance while fasting. The body becomes more efficient at utilizing fat stores, which represent a vast energy reserve compared to limited glycogen stores.

Myth: Fasting is just calorie restriction in disguise. Reality: While calorie reduction may occur with some fasting protocols, the metabolic and hormonal changes triggered by fasting are distinct from those of simple calorie restriction. Fasting affects insulin levels, growth hormone, cellular repair processes, and gene expression in ways that differ from continuous calorie reduction.

Michael found debunking these myths crucial to his

success: "I'd always been told I needed to eat frequently for energy and metabolism. Learning that was largely myth gave me permission to experiment with longer periods without food, which ironically gave me more energy than all the 'energy-sustaining' snacks I'd been consuming."

What Happens In Your Body During Fasting

Understanding the remarkable processes that unfold during fasting can transform how you view those hours without food—from periods of deprivation to windows of incredible cellular activity and renewal. Let's explore what happens in your body during fasting, using accessible language rather than clinical terminology.

When you eat, particularly foods containing carbohydrates, your body converts them into glucose, which enters your bloodstream. This triggers your pancreas to release insulin, the hormone responsible for helping cells absorb glucose for energy or storage. Insulin also signals your body to store excess glucose as glycogen in your liver and muscles, and when those stores are full, to convert additional excess to fat.

As long as insulin levels remain elevated—which happens with frequent eating throughout the day—your body primarily remains in this storage mode, with limited access to fat stores for energy.

When you begin a fasting period, this dynamic changes dramatically:

The First Few Hours (0-4 hours after eating) Your body is digesting and absorbing your most recent meal. Insulin levels are elevated, and your cells are primarily using glucose from this meal for energy.

Early Fasting Stage (4-12 hours after eating) As glucose from your last meal becomes depleted, your body begins accessing stored glycogen from your liver to maintain blood sugar levels. Insulin levels start declining, which sets the stage for fat burning. For many people in modern eating patterns, they rarely get beyond this stage before consuming their next meal.

The Metabolic Switch (12-16 hours after eating) This is where the most interesting transitions occur. As liver glycogen becomes depleted, your body increasingly shifts to burning fat for fuel. This happens through a process called lipolysis, where stored fat is released into the bloodstream as free fatty acids, which are then converted to ketone bodies in the liver. These ketones serve as an alternative energy source for your brain and body.

At the same time, your body begins to upregulate autophagy—the cellular cleaning process mentioned earlier. Think of autophagy as your body's recycling system, breaking down damaged or dysfunctional cellular components and using them to create new, healthy parts. This process helps remove the cellular "junk" that can contribute to aging and disease.

Extended Benefits Stage (16-24 hours) During this period, fat burning and ketone production increase. Many people report experiencing their greatest mental clarity in this stage, as ketones provide a steady, efficient energy source for the brain. Growth hormone levels rise significantly, which helps preserve muscle mass and promotes cellular repair.

Deep Fasting Stage (24-36+ hours) For those practicing longer fasts (which we don't recommend for beginners without appropriate support), autophagy intensifies, and the body continues to adapt to fat-burning mode. Inflammation markers typically decrease, and cellular resilience improves through various adaptive stress responses.

When you eventually break your fast, your body transitions back to using incoming food for energy, and the cycle begins again. However, regular practice of intermittent fasting appears to improve the efficiency of these metabolic switches over time, contributing to better metabolic flexibility.

Michael noticed these changes directly in his experience: "After about three weeks, I could actually feel the difference between running on constant food intake and tapping into my stored energy. The hunger I used to feel was more like withdrawal symptoms —jittery, anxious, urgent. Once my body adapted to fasting, hunger became more of a gentle wave— noticeable but not desperate. And the mental clarity that kicked in around hour 14 or 15 of my fast became something I looked forward to."

Addressing Your Natural Fears

If you're feeling some apprehension about fasting, you're not alone. Concerns about hunger, energy, social situations, and other practical matters are completely normal. Let's address these fears directly with both emotional understanding and practical reassurance.

Fear of Hunger The worry: "I'll be uncomfortable and

distracted by hunger."

The reality: Hunger is not a linear progression that continually intensifies until you eat. Instead, it typically comes in waves that rise and then pass. Many people discover that hunger often diminishes after they've been fasting for a while, as their bodies adjust to accessing stored fat for energy.

Practical approach: During your adaptation period, notice hunger sensations with curiosity rather than fear. You'll likely find that hunger peaks and then subsides, often lasting just 10-20 minutes before easing. Staying hydrated, keeping busy, and reminding yourself that hunger is not an emergency can help manage these sensations until your body adapts.

Fear of Low Energy The worry: "I won't have enough energy for my day."

The reality: While you may experience an adjustment period with some energy fluctuations, many people ultimately report more stable energy throughout the day once adapted to intermittent fasting. This occurs because your body becomes more efficient at accessing fat stores between meals rather than relying solely on regular glucose input.

Practical approach: During your adjustment period, schedule fasting during less demanding times if possible. Begin with shorter fasting periods and gradually extend them as your body adapts. Many find that morning exercise or activity actually helps stabilize energy levels during fasting.

Fear of Social Awkwardness The worry: "How will I

handle social situations that revolve around food?"

The reality: Intermittent fasting can be adapted to accommodate your social life rather than restricting it. The flexibility of most fasting approaches means you can adjust your schedule around important social events.

Practical approach: For special occasions, simply shift your eating window to coincide with social meals. Remember that intermittent fasting is about establishing sustainable rhythms that work for your life, not rigid rules that isolate you from meaningful connections.

Fear of Impacting Health Negatively The worry: "What if fasting isn't healthy for my specific body or condition?"

The reality: While intermittent fasting has shown benefits for many people, individual responses vary based on health status, medications, and other factors. This is why medical consultation is important, particularly for those with existing health conditions.

Practical approach: Start with moderate approaches like 12:12 (12 hours fasting, 12 hours eating) before attempting longer fasting periods. Pay attention to how your body responds and consult healthcare professionals about how fasting might interact with your specific health situation.

Fear of "Doing It Wrong" The worry: "What if I can't follow the protocol perfectly?"

The reality: There is no perfect protocol. Intermittent

fasting is a flexible practice that can be adapted to your body's needs and your lifestyle. The goal is consistency over time, not perfection every day.

Practical approach: Begin with an approach that feels manageable rather than intimidating. Remember that an imperfect practice sustained over time delivers far more benefits than a "perfect" protocol abandoned after a week because it was too restrictive.

Michael wrestled with several of these fears: "I was terrified of being hungry at work presentations. I worried about having enough energy for my morning workouts. What helped most was starting gradually and discovering that many of my fears were based on assumptions that turned out to be wrong. Hunger wasn't as intense or uncomfortable as I'd imagined once my body adapted. And my energy actually improved during fasting once I got through the first couple of weeks."

Try This Now: The Hunger Wave Experiment

This simple experiment can transform how you experience hunger and help you distinguish between true hunger and habitual eating cues.

1. The next time you feel hungry between meals, before automatically reaching for food, pause and commit to observing your hunger for just five minutes.
2. Find a comfortable position either sitting or standing. Close your eyes if that helps you focus inward.
3. Place one hand on your abdomen and take

three deep breaths.
4. Now, with curiosity rather than judgment, direct your attention to the sensation of hunger itself. Where exactly do you feel it in your body? Does it have a shape, size, or intensity? Does it fluctuate or remain constant?
5. For the full five minutes, simply observe these sensations with interest, as if you're a scientist collecting data rather than someone experiencing discomfort.
6. When the five minutes conclude, notice: Has the intensity changed? Has the sensation shifted in any way? Has your emotional response to the hunger changed through observation?

Many people discover through this experiment that hunger isn't the emergency they perceived it to be. They find that simply observing hunger often changes their relationship with it—from something to be immediately resolved to a normal bodily sensation that can be experienced with curiosity.

This small exercise begins building the "hunger muscle"—your capacity to experience hunger without reactivity—which grows stronger with practice. As Michael found: "Learning to sit with hunger for even five minutes changed everything. I realized hunger wasn't dangerous or unbearable—it was just a sensation that came and went like any other."

The Possibility Ahead

As you stand at the threshold of your intermittent

fasting journey, I want you to know that the path ahead offers far more than just potential weight management. You're about to embark on a process of rediscovering your body's innate intelligence and adaptability.

Many who practice intermittent fasting report a profound sense of reclaiming control—not through rigid restriction, but through alignment with their body's natural rhythms. There's freedom in discovering that you don't need to be tethered to regular feeding schedules, that your energy and focus can actually improve during fasting periods, and that hunger is not the emergency our food-abundant culture has conditioned us to believe.

That said, I want to be completely transparent about what to expect. The first week or two of adaptation can present challenges as your body adjusts to new patterns. You may experience hunger pangs, slight energy fluctuations, or even mild irritability as your system recalibrates. These adjustment symptoms are temporary for most people and typically resolve as your body adapts to more efficiently access stored energy between meals.

The key to success is beginning with an approach that feels sustainable for your unique body and lifestyle, then gradually refining your practice based on your personal experience. Intermittent fasting is not about following someone else's perfect protocol but about discovering the rhythm that brings you the greatest well-being and ease.

Michael's journey illustrates this evolution: "I started with a 12-hour overnight fast, which was basically just stopping after dinner and waiting until breakfast. As my body adapted, I gradually extended to 14 hours, then 16. Now I typically fast for 16-18 hours most days, but I remain flexible. Some days I fast longer if it feels right; other days—like celebrations or special occasions—I might shorten or skip my fast entirely. The difference is now I choose based on body awareness rather than habit or social pressure."

Implementation Checklist: Your First Steps

If you're ready to begin exploring intermittent fasting, here are practical first steps:

1. Consult with healthcare providers if you have any existing medical conditions or take medications.
2. Choose a simple starting approach like a 12-hour overnight fast (e.g., finishing dinner by 7pm and eating breakfast no earlier than 7am).
3. Track your current eating patterns for 2-3 days before beginning to establish your baseline habits.
4. Stock your kitchen with foods that will support you during eating windows—focusing on nutritious, satisfying options.
5. Prepare fasting-friendly beverages like water, herbal tea, or black coffee to help manage hunger during fasting periods.
6. Identify potential challenges in your schedule or environment and develop specific strategies to address them.
7. Create a simple tracking system to record fasting periods and notable experiences or

observations.
8. Inform supportive people in your life about your new practice so they can encourage your efforts.
9. Schedule a review point after one week to assess your experience and make any needed adjustments.
10. Approach the process with curiosity rather than rigid expectations, allowing your practice to evolve with your body's feedback.

The principles you've learned in this chapter provide the foundation for everything that follows. Understanding the basic science behind fasting, recognizing the normal adaptation period, and approaching the process with both patience and curiosity will serve you well as you move forward.

In the next chapter, we'll dive deeper into selecting your optimal fasting approach and guide you through your first fasting journey, complete with day-by-day expectations and adjustment strategies. You'll learn how to choose the fasting style that best matches your lifestyle and goals, and how to navigate the initial adaptation period with confidence.

Your body already knows how to fast. It's been waiting for you to simply create the conditions that allow its natural wisdom to flourish.

CHAPTER 2: YOUR FIRST FASTING JOURNEY: GETTING STARTED AND CHOOSING YOUR PATH

The Roadmap Ahead

Embarking on a new health practice often feels like setting off on a journey without a map. You know where you want to go, but the path isn't always clear. This chapter serves as your detailed roadmap for implementing intermittent fasting—from selecting your approach to navigating your first weeks and making necessary adjustments along the way.

Your fasting journey typically follows a predictable progression:

First comes the Preparation Phase, where you gather information, set your intentions, and prepare your environment for success. You're in this phase right now as you read this book.

Next is the Initiation Phase, where you begin your first fasting periods, often with a gentle approach that allows your body to adapt gradually. This usually spans your first 1-2 weeks.

Following this comes the Adaptation Phase, when your body begins adjusting to your new eating pattern. Physical and mental changes become noticeable, and initial challenges begin to subside. This typically occurs between weeks 2-4.

Then you enter the Integration Phase, where fasting becomes more intuitive and comfortable. Benefits become more pronounced, and the practice begins to feel like a natural part of your routine rather than something requiring constant attention. This usually begins around week 4 and continues as your practice matures.

Finally, you reach the Personalization Phase, where you've gained enough experience to fine-tune your approach based on your body's responses, lifestyle needs, and goals. This ongoing phase is where fasting truly becomes your own.

Understanding this general progression can help you contextualize your experiences and recognize that temporary challenges are just that—temporary steps along a longer journey.

The Emotional Landscape of Beginning

Before diving into the practical details, let's acknowledge the emotional terrain of beginning something new, especially when it involves changing your relationship with food. You might be experiencing a complex mix of feelings right now:

Excitement and hope at the possibility of positive changes and benefits you've read about or seen others experience. The prospect of increased energy, mental clarity, or health improvements can be genuinely thrilling.

Apprehension and doubt about whether you can successfully implement this practice or whether it will work for your unique body. Past experiences with diets or health changes might colour your expectations.

Determination and resolve to follow through despite challenges, particularly if you're motivated by specific health goals or concerns.

Uncertainty and confusion about selecting the right approach among many options or about how your body might respond.

Curiosity and interest in the science behind fasting and how your body's natural processes work.

These mixed emotions are not just normal—they're a healthy response to embarking on a meaningful change. Recognizing and accepting these feelings creates a foundation of emotional safety and self-compassion that will serve you throughout your journey.

Rather than expecting unwavering enthusiasm or complete confidence, allow yourself to hold multiple feelings simultaneously. You can be both excited about the benefits ahead and nervous about the challenges. You can be determined to succeed and also uncertain about some aspects of the process.

This emotional awareness isn't just feel-good advice —it's practical strategy. People who acknowledge their mixed feelings about health changes are often more successful than those who try to suppress doubts or fears. By bringing these emotions into conscious awareness, you reduce their power to subtly sabotage your efforts.

Selecting Your First Fasting Approach

One of intermittent fasting's greatest strengths is its flexibility—there are multiple approaches that can deliver benefits. However, this variety can also create confusion for beginners. Let's explore the most common approaches and help you select the one that best aligns with your lifestyle, preferences, and goals.

Time-Restricted Eating (TRE)

This approach involves limiting your daily eating to a specific window of time, creating a consistent fasting period each day.

12:12 (12 hours fasting, 12 hours eating): The gentlest entry point, often involving simply stopping after dinner and waiting until breakfast the next morning. For example, finishing your last bite by 7pm and not eating again until 7am.

14:10 (14 hours fasting, 10 hours eating): A moderate approach that typically involves extending your overnight fast either by delaying breakfast or finishing dinner earlier. For example, eating between 9am and 7pm only.

16:8 (16 hours fasting, 8 hours eating): One of the most popular approaches, often implemented by skipping breakfast and eating lunch, dinner, and perhaps a snack within an 8-hour window, such as 12pm to 8pm.

18:6 or 20:4 (18 or 20 hours fasting, 6 or 4 hours eating): More advanced approaches typically adopted after gaining experience with shorter fasting windows.

TRE is ideal if you:

1. Prefer consistency in your daily routine
2. Want to practice fasting every day
3. Find it easier to maintain one ongoing pattern rather than alternating approaches
4. Have regular work and social schedules

Modified Alternate-Day Approaches

These approaches involve alternating between days of regular eating and days with significant calorie reduction or complete fasting.

5:2 Method: Eat normally five days per week and reduce calories significantly (typically to about 500-600) on two non-consecutive days. This creates two modified fasting days each week.

Alternate-Day Modified Fasting: Alternate between days of normal eating and days with significant calorie reduction (again, typically 500-600 calories).

These approaches work well if you:

1. Prefer having full days where you eat normally without timing restrictions
2. Find it easier to limit calories dramatically for a full day rather than stopping eating earlier each day

3. Have a flexible schedule that allows for lower-energy days
4. Want to practice significant calorie restriction less frequently than daily

24-Hour Protocols

These involve completing one or two full 24-hour fasts per week.

Weekly 24-Hour Fast: Choose one day per week to complete a 24-hour fast, such as finishing dinner at 6pm on Tuesday and not eating again until dinner at 6pm on Wednesday.

Twice-Weekly 24-Hour Fasts: Similar to the above but implemented twice weekly on non-consecutive days.

These approaches suit you if you:

1. Want maximum flexibility during most of your week
2. Can dedicate specific days to more intensive fasting
3. Prefer fewer but longer fasting periods rather than daily restrictions
4. Have experience with shorter fasts and want to explore extended benefits

The On-Ramp Approach (Recommended for Most Beginners)

For most people new to fasting, I recommend what I call the "on-ramp approach"—a gradual progression that allows your body and mind to adapt comfortably:

Week 1: Begin with a 12-hour overnight fast (e.g., 7pm to 7am), which many people already do naturally without calling it "fasting."

Weeks 2-3: Extend to 14 hours if the 12-hour window feels comfortable, perhaps 7pm to 9am.

Weeks 4+: If desired and if your body has adapted well, extend to 16 hours for some or all days, such as 7pm to 11am or 6pm to 10am.

This gradual progression honours your body's need for adaptation and builds confidence through successful experiences. Rather than diving into the deep end, you're giving your metabolism, hunger hormones, and daily habits time to adjust.

Decision Point: Finding Your Fasting Fit

To select your optimal starting approach, consider these questions:

1. What is your primary goal with intermittent fasting?
   a. Health improvements beyond weight loss
   b. Weight management
   c. Mental clarity and focus
   d. Simplifying your relationship with food
   e. Other specific goals
2. Which matters more to you—consistency or intensity?
   a. I prefer doing something moderate

every day (suggests TRE)
   b. I prefer more intensive practices less frequently (suggests alternate-day approaches)

3. When during the day do you most need mental clarity and energy?
   a. Mornings (suggests eating earlier in the day, fasting evenings)
   b. Afternoons (suggests either approach could work)
   c. Evenings (suggests fasting mornings, eating later)

4. How does your hunger typically manifest?
   a. Strongest in mornings (suggests eating earlier in the day)
   b. Strongest in evenings (suggests eating later in the day)
   c. Consistent throughout the day (focus on other factors for decision)

5. What does your social and work schedule require?
   a. Regular social meals (align eating window with these occasions)
   b. Work meetings involving food (consider which can be navigated without eating)
   c. Family meals (determine which are most important to participate in)

6. How would you describe your previous experience with hunger?
   a. Very uncomfortable, anxiety-

producing (start with gentler approaches)
b. Manageable but still concerning (start with moderate approaches)
c. Interesting, not particularly troublesome (could start with standard approaches)

7. How would you rate your current metabolic health?
    a. Concerns like blood sugar issues, insulin resistance (start very gradually)
    b. Generally healthy but some concerns (start with moderate approaches)
    c. Excellent metabolic health (could start with standard approaches)

One Person's Decision Process

Let me share how Lisa, a 38-year-old marketing manager and mother of two, worked through selecting her optimal fasting approach. Her case illustrates how personal factors can guide this decision.

Lisa's primary goals were increasing mental focus at work and managing her weight, which had crept up over the past few years. She noticed her energy crashing around 3pm each day, making afternoon work challenging. She had a regular schedule with most workdays looking similar: getting kids to school by 8am, working until 5pm, and family dinner around 6:30pm.

"I knew myself well enough to recognize that I'd need

a consistent daily approach rather than alternating between different patterns on different days," Lisa explained. "I function best with routine, so time-restricted eating seemed the logical choice."

Next, she considered her hunger patterns. "I've never been a breakfast person—often just grabbing coffee and maybe toast while rushing with the kids. But by late morning I'd be starving and distracted. Then after eating lunch, I'd feel sluggish for about an hour."

Looking at her social and family commitments, dinner with her family was non-negotiable. "Those evening meals are when we connect as a family. I wasn't willing to miss that."

Lisa also considered her experience with hunger. "Hunger had always felt urgent to me—like an emergency I needed to fix immediately. The idea of extending periods without food seemed challenging but also intriguing."

After weighing these factors, Lisa decided to start with a 14:10 approach, eating between 11am and 9pm. This allowed her to skip breakfast (which she wasn't enjoying anyway), have lunch with colleagues, maintain family dinner, and occasionally have an evening snack if needed.

"What surprised me was how the structure actually freed me," she said. "Instead of thinking about food all morning, I knew I wasn't eating until 11am, so I could focus completely on work. I also found that delaying my first meal meant I wasn't starving by mid-morning like I used to be when I had toast at 7am."

After three weeks, Lisa naturally shifted to a 16:8 pattern, eating between 12pm and 8pm, as her body adapted and morning hunger diminished. This timing gave her even more focused morning work time while still preserving family dinners.

The key lesson from Lisa's experience isn't the specific schedule she chose, but the thoughtful consideration of her unique circumstances, preferences, and non-negotiables. Your optimal approach will reflect your own distinct needs and lifestyle.

Your First Week: What to Expect Day by Day

The first week of intermittent fasting often sets the tone for your entire practice. Let's walk through what you might experience day by day, with both the physical sensations and emotional responses you might encounter.

Day 1: The Beginning

Physical experience: Your first day might feel surprisingly easy, as novelty and motivation are high. You might notice mild hunger during your usual eating times if you're skipping or delaying meals. Some people experience slight headaches, particularly if reducing caffeine or sugar simultaneously.

Emotional experience: Excitement and determination typically characterize this day. You'll likely feel optimistic and eager to experience the benefits you've read about.

Helpful strategy: Start on a day when you have control

over your schedule and fewer demands. Have plenty of water, herbal tea, or black coffee available to sip during fasting periods. Remind yourself that any discomfort is temporary and part of the adaptation process.

Day 2: The Reality Check

Physical experience: As the novelty diminishes, you might notice hunger more prominently. Your body, accustomed to eating at certain times, will produce hunger hormones on that schedule. Some people experience mild light-headedness if standing quickly.

Emotional experience: Doubt often creeps in on day two. "Can I really do this?" or "Is this really worth it?" thoughts are completely normal as the initial excitement gives way to the reality of changing established patterns.

Helpful strategy: Distraction works wonders on this day. Schedule engaging activities during your usual eating times. Remind yourself that hunger is not an emergency and typically passes within 20 minutes if you don't respond to it. Stay well-hydrated and add a pinch of salt to your water if you feel light-headed.

Day 3: The Challenge Point

Physical experience: Many people find day three the most physically challenging. Hunger may feel more intense, and some experience mild fatigue, irritability, or headaches as their bodies adapt to using stored energy rather than constant food intake.

Emotional experience: Frustration and impatience are common. You may question whether benefits are worth the discomfort you're experiencing.

Helpful strategy: This is the day to practice extreme self-care. Ensure adequate hydration, consider a pinch of high-quality salt in water for electrolytes, and get sufficient rest. Remind yourself that day three is often the turning point—many report improvements beginning shortly after this challenging day.

Day 4: The First Glimpse

Physical experience: Many begin noticing initial positive changes on day four. Morning hunger often starts decreasing, and some report their first experiences of heightened mental clarity. Energy may begin stabilizing as your body becomes more efficient at accessing stored fat.

Emotional experience: Cautious optimism typically emerges. While challenges remain, the first hints of benefits provide motivation to continue.

Helpful strategy: Begin noting positive changes, however subtle. Maybe your energy is slightly more stable, or you're thinking less about food. These early wins, when recognized, build momentum and reinforcement.

Day 5: Building Consistency

Physical experience: Bodies differ in adaptation speed, but by day five, many notice decreased hunger intensity, particularly during the morning hours. Some experience improved digestion or less bloating as the digestive system gets more rest between meals.

Emotional experience: Growing confidence characterizes this stage for most people. The practice starts feeling more sustainable as initial hurdles diminish.

Helpful strategy: Begin noticing how your energy flows throughout the day. Are there times when you feel particularly clear and focused? Times when hunger is most manageable? This awareness helps you refine your approach.

Day 6: Testing Flexibility

Physical experience: By day six, physical adaptation is progressing well for most people. Hunger patterns become more predictable, and energy often improves. Some notice changes in taste perception—food often tastes more vibrant and satisfying when breaking a fast.

Emotional experience: A sense of accomplishment starts building. Many begin feeling empowered by their increasing ability to work with hunger rather than immediately responding to it.

Helpful strategy: If your schedule allows, test slight variations in your fasting timing to discover what works best. If you've been fasting 14 hours, try 15. If you've been breaking your fast at 11am, try 11:30am and notice any differences in your experience.

Day 7: Reflection Point

Physical experience: While still early in the adaptation process, by the end of week one many people report more stable energy levels, decreased hunger, and improved sleep quality. The body is beginning to adjust to new patterns.

Emotional experience: Pride in completing a full week combines with curiosity about continuing benefits. Many experience a new sense of freedom from the constant pull of food and eating schedules.

Helpful strategy: Take time to reflect on your full week's experience. What worked well? What challenges remain? What surprised you? This reflection helps you make informed adjustments for week two.

Breakthrough Moments: What to Watch For

While everyone's experience is unique, certain breakthrough moments commonly occur during the early weeks of intermittent fasting. Recognizing these moments can provide tremendous encouragement and reinforce your practice:

The Hunger Wave: The first time you notice hunger arise and then pass without eating is often surprising and liberating. Many describe this as the moment they realized hunger isn't an emergency that must be immediately addressed but rather a wave that rises and falls.

The Morning Clarity: Many practitioners remember the first morning they experience unusual mental sharpness and focus during their fasting period. This often feels like a fog lifting, revealing a level of cognitive clarity they hadn't experienced before.

The Energy Stability: After years of energy crashes

and afternoon slumps, many find profound relief when they first notice sustained energy throughout the day without the dramatic peaks and valleys they'd previously considered normal.

The Spontaneous Extension: The first time you naturally extend your fasting window because you simply aren't hungry yet is a powerful moment. It represents your body's growing metabolic flexibility and changing relationship with hunger cues.

The Food Freedom: Many recall the precise moment they realized they were no longer thinking about food constantly. This mental space and freedom from food preoccupation often comes as a surprising and welcome side effect.

The Mindful Meal: The experience of truly tasting your food—perhaps noticing flavours and textures you previously missed—often marks a transition to more mindful, satisfying eating within your eating windows.

The Body Trust: Perhaps the most profound breakthrough is when you first sense a growing trust in your body's signals and wisdom. This might manifest as recognizing true hunger versus habitual eating, or as newfound confidence in your body's ability to function well during fasting.

Lisa recalled her first major breakthrough clearly: "It was day nine, and I was in a meeting that ran long, pushing past my usual 12pm eating time. In the past, I would have been anxiously watching the clock, distracted by hunger. But I suddenly realized I was fully engaged in the discussion, not thinking about food at all. My body was completely fine continuing the fast for another hour. That's when I knew something fundamental had shifted."

Troubleshooting Guide for Common First-Week Challenges

Even with perfect preparation, challenges naturally arise as you adjust to intermittent fasting. Here are solutions for the most common issues beginners face:

Challenge: Intense Hunger *If you experience hunger that feels overwhelming or makes it difficult to function...*

1. Try consuming a pinch of high-quality salt in water, as electrolyte balance affects hunger signals
2. Ensure adequate hydration, as thirst can masquerade as hunger
3. Consume black coffee or plain tea, which can blunt hunger temporarily for many people
4. If hunger persists intensely, consider shortening your fasting window temporarily as your body adapts
5. Remember that hunger typically comes in waves that pass within 15-20 minutes

Challenge: Headaches *If you develop headaches during your fasting period...*

1. Check hydration—many fasting headaches result from inadequate fluid intake
2. Address electrolyte balance with a pinch of salt in water
3. If you're reducing caffeine simultaneously,

headaches may be withdrawal-related; consider maintaining normal caffeine intake initially and reducing gradually after establishing your fasting practice
4. Break your fast if headaches become severe or persistent

Challenge: Light-headedness or Dizziness *If you experience dizziness, especially when standing quickly...*

1. Add electrolytes to your water (sodium, potassium, magnesium)
2. Stand up slowly, giving your body time to adjust
3. Consider whether your fasting window is too long for your current adaptation level
4. Break your fast with easily digestible nutrients if symptoms persist
5. Consult your healthcare provider if dizziness is recurring or severe

Challenge: Sleep Disturbances *If you notice changes in your sleep quality...*

1. Avoid fasting approaches that leave you hungry at bedtime
2. Consider timing your last meal 2-3 hours before sleep
3. Try consuming most of your carbohydrates with your final meal of the day
4. For women especially, very low carbohydrate intake can sometimes disrupt sleep; ensure adequate carbohydrate consumption during your eating window

Challenge: Afternoon Energy Crashes *If you experience significant energy dips during specific times...*

1. Examine whether your eating window might be better aligned with your natural energy fluctuations
2. Consider breaking your fast earlier if crashes occur before your first meal
3. Ensure your first meal includes protein, healthy fats, and fibre for stable blood sugar
4. Temporary energy fluctuations are normal during adaptation; many resolve within 2-3 weeks

Challenge: Digestive Changes *If you notice changes in digestion or bowel movements...*

1. Remember that fewer meals naturally leads to less frequent bowel movements, which isn't necessarily problematic
2. Ensure adequate hydration during fasting periods
3. Include sufficient fibre during eating windows
4. Give your digestive system time to adjust to new patterns

Challenge: Social Pressure *If you face questions or pressure from others about your eating pattern...*

1. Prepare simple, non-defensive responses like "I'm exploring what works best for my body" or "I'm trying a new eating schedule that's helping my energy"
2. Remind yourself that your health choices don't

require external validation or approval
3. Consider flexibility for special social occasions while maintaining your regular pattern most days
4. Find social activities that don't centre around food during your fasting periods

Challenge: Breaking Fast Impulsively *If you find yourself breaking your fast earlier than planned without clear reason...*

1. Examine whether your fasting window might be too ambitious for your current adaptation level
2. Create specific routines for challenging time periods
3. Practice mindfulness techniques when urges arise
4. Plan a specific, nourishing meal for breaking your fast to increase motivation

Adjusting Your Approach: Flexibility, Not Failure

One of the most important skills for successful intermittent fasting is the ability to make thoughtful adjustments based on your experience. Many beginners mistake necessary adaptation for failure, abandoning their practice entirely when simple modifications would solve their challenges.

The key is distinguishing between normal adaptation discomfort and signs that your approach needs adjustment. Here's how to know the difference:

Normal adaptation experiences that typically resolve

with time and persistence include:
1. Initial hunger during usual meal times that diminishes within 1-3 weeks
2. Mild headaches in the first week that gradually subside
3. Temporary energy fluctuations that stabilize as your body becomes more efficient at fat-burning
4. Slight digestive changes as your system adjusts to new eating patterns
5. Mild mood fluctuations that typically improve as energy stabilizes

Signs that your approach needs adjustment include:
1. Persistent intense hunger that doesn't diminish after 1-2 weeks
2. Recurring headaches or dizziness that don't improve with hydration and electrolytes
3. Significant negative impacts on your mood, energy, or cognitive function
4. Disrupted sleep that persists beyond the initial adaptation phase
5. Difficulty maintaining normal daily activities due to fasting symptoms

If you notice these adjustment signals, consider these modifications:
1. Shorten your fasting window temporarily. If you've started with 16:8, try 14:10 for a week or two before gradually extending again.
2. Change your fasting/eating window timing. Some people do better with morning eating and afternoon/evening fasting, while others prefer the reverse.

3. Examine what you're consuming during eating windows. Insufficient protein, healthy fats, and fibre can make fasting periods more difficult.
4. Assess whether your calorie intake during eating windows is adequate. Intermittent fasting shouldn't mean severe caloric restriction.
5. Consider whether you're making too many dietary changes simultaneously. Changing both when and what you eat at the same time can overwhelm your adaptation capacity.

Lisa's experience illustrates thoughtful adjustment: "I initially tried stopping eating at 7pm, but found myself really hungry in the evenings when I was relaxing with my family. Rather than abandoning my practice, I shifted my window to 11am-9pm instead of 10am-6pm. That small change made it sustainable for me while still providing a 14-hour fast."

Remember that adjustments aren't failures—they're intelligent responses to your body's feedback. The goal isn't rigid adherence to your initial plan but rather finding the approach that works best for your unique body and lifestyle.

Journaling Prompts for Your First Week

Reflection accelerates learning. These journaling prompts help you develop greater body awareness and identify patterns specific to your experience:

Before starting your practice:
1. What are my main hopes and concerns about

beginning intermittent fasting?
2. How would I describe my current relationship with hunger?
3. What patterns have I noticed about when my energy is highest and lowest throughout the day?
4. What will success look like for me after one week? After one month?

Daily reflections during week one:
1. How did my energy flow throughout the day?
2. What hunger sensations did I notice, and how did they change throughout fasting periods?
3. What emotions came up around fasting today?
4. What went well today? What was challenging?
5. What am I learning about my body's signals and patterns?

End of first week reflection:
1. What surprised me most about this first week?
2. How has my experience of hunger changed, if at all?
3. What benefits have I noticed, even subtle ones?
4. What challenges remain that I'd like to address?
5. What adjustments might make this practice more sustainable for me?
6. What am I proud of accomplishing this week?

Lisa found journaling particularly valuable: "Writing about my experience made me notice patterns I would have missed otherwise—like how my afternoon slump disappeared by day five, or how my hunger had a predictable peak around 10am but would fade if I just waited it out. These observations gave me confidence that the process was working even when changes were subtle."

Looking Ahead: Building on Your Foundation

As you complete your first week, you're establishing a foundation that will support your entire fasting journey. The body awareness, troubleshooting skills, and adaptation capacity you're developing now will serve you well as your practice matures.

In the coming weeks, you can expect:

1. Increasingly stable energy as your metabolic flexibility improves
2. More predictable hunger patterns that feel less urgent
3. Growing confidence in distinguishing true hunger from habitual eating cues
4. Improved ability to adjust your approach based on daily needs and circumstances
5. Deeper appreciation for how your unique body responds to fasting

The most successful practitioners approach intermittent fasting with a blend of consistency and flexibility—maintaining their core practice while adapting to life's natural variations. Some days you might extend your fast if you're feeling good and your schedule allows; other days you might shorten it for special occasions or unusual energy needs.

Lisa reflected on her evolving approach: "After six weeks, I had settled into a comfortable 16:8 pattern most days, eating between noon and 8pm. But I discovered I actually felt better with a shorter fast before particularly demanding workdays, so I adapted to eating breakfast on those mornings. What had initially felt like a strict protocol became a flexible tool I could adjust based on my body's needs and my life's demands."

Implementation Checklist: First Week Success

Use this checklist to prepare for and navigate your first week of intermittent fasting:

1. Select your starting approach based on your lifestyle, preferences, and previous experience with hunger.
2. Choose a start date that doesn't coincide with major events, travel, or unusual stress.
3. Prepare your environment by stocking fasting-friendly beverages and planning nourishing meals for your eating windows.
4. Inform supportive people about your new practice so they can encourage rather than inadvertently undermine your efforts.
5. Clear your schedule of food-centred social events during your first week if possible, or plan flexible approaches for these occasions.
6. Establish a simple tracking method to record fasting periods and notable experiences (a journal, app, or simple calendar notation).
7. Create contingency plans for common challenges like unexpected hunger, social pressure, or energy dips.
8. Set up environmental cues that support your

practice, such as putting away kitchen items during fasting periods or preparing water bottles for the morning.
9. Plan specific self-care practices for challenging moments during your adaptation phase.
10. Schedule your week-one review to reflect on your experience and make any needed adjustments.
11. Begin with self-compassion, remembering that adaptation is a process, not an event.

Your first week of intermittent fasting represents the beginning of a profound shift in your relationship with food, hunger, and your body's natural rhythms. By selecting an approach aligned with your unique needs, preparing thoughtfully for challenges, and maintaining flexibility as you learn from experience, you're setting the stage for sustainable success.

In the next chapter, we'll explore how to optimize what you eat during your eating windows, manage hydration during fasting periods, and develop a healthier emotional relationship with food—all essential components of a successful intermittent fasting practice.

Remember that each day of practice builds your "fasting muscle"—your capacity to work with hunger skillfully, access stored energy efficiently, and maintain metabolic flexibility. The challenges of this first week are temporary, while the skills and awareness you're developing will serve you for a lifetime.

CHAPTER 3: FOOD, DRINK, AND THE SCIENCE OF YOUR BODY

Transforming Your Relationship with Food

One of the most surprising and profound effects of intermittent fasting isn't just when you eat, but how your entire experience of food transforms. Many practitioners discover that their relationship with eating evolves in unexpected and welcome ways.

Consider David's experience. A busy attorney in his mid-forties, David had always treated food functionally—something consumed quickly between meetings or late at night after a long day. "I ate without thinking," he reflected. "Food was fuel, often consumed while working or driving. I barely tasted what I ate."

After just three weeks of practicing intermittent fasting with a daily 16-hour fast, David noticed something remarkable: "When I broke my fast with lunch, I found myself actually tasting my food—noticing flavours I'd never detected before. Without realizing it, I started eating more slowly and feeling satisfied with less. Food became something to experience rather than just consume."

This transformation represents more than just a nice side effect. It reflects profound changes in how your body and brain process food when given regular periods of digestive rest. As your body shifts between fed and fasted states, your taste perception sharpens, your appreciation for subtle flavours increases, and your satisfaction from appropriate portions deepens. Many report a natural gravitation toward more nutritious foods—not from force of will, but from genuine preference as their palates recalibrate.

Perhaps most significantly, many practitioners discover a decrease in food's emotional power over them. The urgent need to eat in response to stress, boredom, or other emotions often diminishes as fasting creates both physical and psychological space between stimulus and response.

These changes don't happen immediately for everyone, but they represent a common evolution as your fasting practice matures. Let's explore the fascinating science behind these transformations and how they can help you optimize your fasting experience.

The Science of Fed and Fasted States

To truly understand intermittent fasting's power, we need to explore what happens in your body during both fed and fasted states. Rather than describing these processes with technical terminology, let's use more accessible language and metaphors to bring these remarkable mechanisms to life.

Imagine your body as a sophisticated hybrid vehicle with two distinct energy systems:

The Fed State: Your Body's "Immediate Consumption" System

When you eat, particularly foods containing carbohydrates, your body converts them to glucose, which enters your bloodstream. This rising blood sugar triggers your pancreas to release insulin—a hormone that acts like a key, unlocking cells so they can absorb this glucose for immediate energy use or storage.

In this fed state, your body preferentially uses incoming food energy while storing excess. Think of it as operating in "storage mode"—with insulin levels elevated, your body efficiently packs away nutrients for future use. Excess glucose gets stored first as glycogen in your liver and muscles (about 1-2 days' worth of energy), and once those stores are full, additional excess is converted to body fat.

During the fed state, your body also focuses on growth processes. Insulin signals cells to build and expand—constructing new proteins, repairing tissues, and growing. This state is essential for replenishment and building, but problems arise when we remain perpetually in this state through constant eating.

In our modern food environment, many people spend nearly all their waking hours in the fed state—eating from soon after waking until shortly before bed, with regular meals and snacks throughout the day. This constant fed state keeps insulin levels chronically elevated, which over time can lead to insulin resistance and limited access to stored fat for energy.

The Fasted State: Your Body's "Access and Clean" System

When you stop eating for a period of time, insulin levels gradually decline as your blood glucose returns to baseline. As insulin drops, a remarkable transition occurs—your body shifts from primarily storing energy to accessing stored energy.

First, your body taps into liver glycogen (stored glucose) to maintain blood sugar levels. This process typically sustains you for 8-12 hours after your last meal, which is why many people who eat dinner and then breakfast never fully enter the deeper fasted state.

Once liver glycogen becomes depleted, your body increasingly turns to its fat stores for energy. Fat cells release stored fatty acids, which your liver converts into ketones—an alternative fuel source that can power most cells in your body, including your brain. This metabolic flexibility—the ability to smoothly transition between burning glucose and fat—represents a cornerstone of metabolic health that many modern humans have lost through constant eating.

But the fasted state involves much more than just burning fat. It activates a fascinating cellular cleaning process called autophagy, which deserves special attention.

Autophagy: Your Cellular Cleanup Crew

The term autophagy literally means "self-eating," but don't let that sound alarming. This normal bodily process involves your cells identifying old, damaged, or dysfunctional components and recycling them—breaking them down and using the parts to build new, healthy cellular structures.

Think of autophagy as your body's built-in renovation system. Just as a responsible homeowner periodically inspects their house, identifies damaged materials, removes them, and replaces them with fresh materials, your cells use fasting periods to conduct this essential maintenance.

Dr. Yoshinori Ohsumi received the 2016 Nobel Prize in Medicine for his groundbreaking work on autophagy mechanisms. His research revealed how this process helps remove damaged proteins, reinvigorate mitochondria (your cells' energy powerhouses), and even eliminate potential cancer-causing mutations. Autophagy appears to play crucial roles in longevity, disease resistance, and overall cellular health.

Autophagy occurs naturally during fasted states, particularly as fasts extend beyond 14-16 hours. When insulin levels drop and cellular energy becomes slightly restricted, your cells receive signals to begin this cleaning and renewal process. It's as if your body says, "We don't have new materials coming in right now, so let's use this time to clean house and recycle what we can."

This cellular cleanup may contribute to many of fasting's observed benefits—from improved mental clarity to potentially reduced risk of neurodegenerative diseases and certain cancers. While autophagy happens to some degree during sleep, extending the fasting period amplifies this beneficial process.

Metabolic Switching: The Key to Adaptation

The ability to transition smoothly between these two

states—fed and fasted—represents what researchers call "metabolic flexibility." This evolutionary adaptation allowed humans to thrive through periods of feast and famine. Our ancestors might not have eaten for extended periods while hunting or during seasonal food scarcity, yet they maintained energy and cognitive function.

Dr. Mark Mattson, a neuroscientist formerly with the National Institute on Aging and now at Johns Hopkins University, describes this as "metabolic switching"—the regular cycling between glucose and ketone metabolism. His research suggests this switching itself, rather than continuous ketosis or continuous glucose metabolism, may drive many of fasting's benefits.

This cyclical pattern—moving between fed and fasted states—appears to trigger adaptive stress responses that make cells more resilient. It's similar to how exercise works: the temporary stress of exercise stimulates adaptations that make your muscles and cardiovascular system stronger. Similarly, the mild stress of fasting periods triggers cellular resilience mechanisms that wouldn't activate if we remained perpetually fed.

David noticed this adaptation directly: "After about three weeks, I could feel when my body switched fuel sources. I'd feel a clear transition around hour 14 of fasting—my thinking would sharpen, and a subtle but noticeable energy would kick in. It's completely different from the jittery energy of coffee or sugar. It feels clean and steady."

Try This Now: The Flavour Awakening Experiment

This simple experiment helps you experience firsthand how fasting can enhance your taste perception and food appreciation.

1. Select a small piece of high-quality dark chocolate (or another food with complex flavour notes).
2. On a day when you've been eating regularly throughout the morning, taste the chocolate in the afternoon. As you eat it, pay close attention to the flavour complexity, sweetness level, and your overall enjoyment. Rate these aspects on a scale of 1-10 and make brief notes about your experience.
3. Two days later, taste the same chocolate to break a fast of at least 14 hours (for example, after fasting overnight and through the morning). Again, rate the flavour complexity, sweetness level, and overall enjoyment on the same scale.
4. Compare your two experiences. Many people discover that food tastes significantly more flavourful, complex, and satisfying when breaking a fast compared to eating in an already-fed state.

This experiment often reveals why many long-term fasting practitioners report greater satisfaction from their meals despite eating less frequently. The sensory experience becomes richer, making quality more important than quantity. As David noted: "I'm spending less on food overall because I'm eating fewer times a day, but I now spend more on higher-quality foods because I can actually taste the difference."

Nutritional Considerations During Eating Windows

While intermittent fasting focuses primarily on when you eat rather than what you eat, the composition of your meals during eating windows significantly impacts your fasting experience, overall health outcomes, and long-term sustainability. Let's explore how to optimize your nutrition while maintaining a healthy, non-restrictive relationship with food.

Breaking Your Fast Optimally

The first meal after a fast deserves special attention, as it sets the metabolic tone for your eating window and affects how you'll feel during your next fasting period.

When breaking a fast, especially longer ones (16+ hours), consider these principles:

1. Start moderately: Begin with a reasonable portion rather than an excessive meal. Your digestive system has been resting and will respond better to a measured reintroduction of food.
2. Include protein: Starting with protein helps rebuild tissues that may have undergone repair during your fast and provides lasting satiety. Good options include eggs, Greek yogurt, fish, poultry, tofu, or legumes.
3. Add healthy fats: Including sources like avocado, olive oil, nuts, or seeds helps maintain satiety, supports hormone production, and provides essential fatty acids.

4. Incorporate fibre-rich foods: Vegetables, fruits, and whole grains provide necessary fibre for digestive health and help stabilize blood sugar response.
5. Consider limiting simple carbohydrates: Breaking your fast with high amounts of simple carbs or sugar can cause a sharp insulin response that might leave you hungry again quickly.

David's experience with fast-breaking meals evolved over time: "I used to break my fast with whatever was convenient—often a sandwich or pasta. I'd feel energetic for an hour, then crash hard. When I switched to breaking my fast with eggs, avocado, and vegetables, the difference was remarkable. I stayed satisfied longer, and my energy remained stable throughout the afternoon."

For longer fasts (24+ hours), which are more advanced practices, breaking your fast becomes even more important. In these cases, starting with a small, easily digestible meal and waiting 30-60 minutes before consuming a larger meal helps ease your digestive system back into processing food.

Nutritional Balance During Eating Windows

Within your eating window, aim for nutritional completeness and balance rather than restriction. Some basic principles to consider:

Adequate protein: Consuming sufficient protein—generally 0.8-1.2 grams per kilogram of body weight daily for most adults—supports muscle maintenance, satiety, and overall health. This becomes especially important when eating fewer meals, as each meal needs to provide more substantial nutrition.

Micronutrient density: When consuming fewer eating occasions, the nutritional quality of your meals becomes more critical. Focus on including a variety of colourful vegetables, fruits, whole grains, lean proteins, and healthy fats to ensure you get the full spectrum of vitamins, minerals, and phytonutrients your body needs.

Fiber adequacy: Sufficient fibre intake supports digestive health, feeds beneficial gut bacteria, and helps maintain satiety. Aim to include fibre-rich foods like vegetables, fruits, legumes, and whole grains in your meals.

Carbohydrate consideration: Your optimal carbohydrate intake depends on your activity level, metabolic health, and personal response. Active individuals typically benefit from more carbohydrates, while those with insulin resistance may do better with moderate carbohydrate intake. Pay attention to how different carbohydrate levels affect your hunger and energy during fasting periods.

Caloric sufficiency: Intermittent fasting shouldn't mean severe caloric restriction. During your eating window, ensure you're consuming enough energy to support your body's needs. Chronically undereating can lead to nutritional deficiencies, hormonal disruptions, and sustainability challenges.

Finding Your Food Balance

Rather than prescribing exact meals or rigid macronutrient ratios, I encourage discovering what works best for your unique body through mindful experimentation. Pay attention to:

1. How different meals affect your energy during both fed and fasted states
2. Which foods leave you feeling satisfied versus triggering cravings
3. How your digestion responds to various food combinations
4. Which meals help you sleep better and wake refreshed
5. How your food choices affect your next day's hunger levels

David's approach reflected this personalized discovery: "I realized that moderately higher protein and fat with dinner helped me sleep better and feel less hungry the next morning. But if I ate too heavy a dinner, especially with lots of refined carbs, I'd wake up feeling sluggish. It took some experimentation, but I found my personal balance."

This mindful approach to eating helps transform intermittent fasting from a temporary diet into a sustainable lifestyle. By discovering the foods that best support your unique physiology and preferences, you develop a naturally healthy eating pattern that requires less willpower and provides greater satisfaction.

Hydration, Electrolytes, and Beverages During Fasting

Proper hydration plays a crucial role in successful

fasting, affecting everything from hunger levels to energy and cognitive function. Understanding what to drink—and what to avoid—during fasting periods can significantly enhance your experience.

Water: Your Fasting Foundation

Water should form the cornerstone of your fasting hydration strategy. During fasting periods, many people become more aware of their body's genuine thirst signals, which were previously often confused with hunger.

Aim to drink water regularly throughout your fasting window. While individual needs vary based on body size, activity level, and climate, a general guideline is 2-3 litres (about 8-12 cups) daily for most adults. Your urine should be light yellow to clear for optimal hydration.

Many find that slight flavour enhancements make adequate hydration easier to maintain. Consider adding:

1. A slice of lemon or lime
2. A few cucumber slices
3. A sprig of fresh mint
4. A splash of apple cider vinegar (which may also have modest benefits for blood sugar management)

These additions provide taste without significantly affecting your fasted state.

Electrolytes: The Missing Link

Electrolytes—minerals like sodium, potassium, magnesium, and calcium—play essential roles in hydration, nerve function, muscle contraction, and overall cellular health. During fasting, particularly as your body depletes glycogen stores, you excrete more water and electrolytes, potentially leading to imbalances.

Common signs of electrolyte imbalance during fasting include:

1. Headaches
2. Dizziness
3. Muscle cramps
4. Fatigue
5. Irritability
6. Heart palpitations

Many beginners attribute these symptoms to hunger when they're actually experiencing electrolyte depletion. Adding a pinch of high-quality salt to your water or consuming electrolyte supplements without calories (avoid those with added sugars) can often resolve these issues quickly.

David found this adjustment transformative: "The headaches I experienced during my first week of fasting completely disappeared when I started adding a pinch of sea salt to my morning water. It was like flipping a switch—suddenly fasting became much more comfortable."

Fasting-Friendly Beverages

Beyond water, several beverages can support your

fasting practice without breaking your fast:

Black coffee: Unsweetened black coffee contains negligible calories and won't trigger significant insulin release. Many find it helps suppress hunger and enhances mental clarity during fasting. Coffee may also stimulate autophagy, potentially enhancing fasting's cellular benefits.

Plain tea: Black, green, white, and herbal teas (unsweetened) are generally considered fast-compatible. Different varieties offer various benefits—green tea contains compounds that may support fat metabolism, while certain herbal teas can help manage hunger or provide calming effects.

Sparkling water: Unflavoured or naturally flavoured without sweeteners, sparkling water can add interest to your hydration routine without affecting your fasted state.

Bone broth: For longer fasts (24+ hours), some protocols permit small amounts of bone broth to provide electrolytes and minimal nutrition while maintaining most fasting benefits. This represents a more modified approach and may be appropriate for those needing additional support during extended fasts.

What Breaks a Fast?

Understanding what constitutes "breaking a fast" requires nuance, as the answer depends partly on your fasting goals:

For metabolic health and insulin sensitivity: Any

calories, particularly carbohydrates or proteins that trigger insulin, technically break a fast. Even small amounts of cream in coffee, while minimally caloric, will stimulate some insulin release.

For autophagy benefits: The threshold is less clear, but generally, protein consumption most significantly blunts autophagy, while trace amounts of fat may have less impact.

For practical sustainability: Many experienced practitioners adopt a more flexible definition that allows minimal additions (like a splash of milk in coffee) if these significantly enhance their ability to maintain fasting consistently over time.

For weight management: Very small caloric additions (under 50 calories) likely won't significantly impact weight-related outcomes if they help you maintain your overall fasting schedule.

The key is intentionality—understanding the potential effects of various additions and making informed decisions aligned with your primary goals.

Decision Point: Selecting Your Optimal Fasting Beverages

To determine your ideal hydration strategy during fasting periods, consider these questions:

1. What is your primary goal with intermittent fasting?
    a. Metabolic health/insulin sensitivity (strictest approach to fasting purity)
    b. Weight management (moderate

flexibility may be acceptable)
   c. Autophagy/cellular cleansing (caution with proteins and significant calories)
   d. Digestive rest (avoid anything requiring significant digestion)
   e. Overall lifestyle improvement (may allow strategic flexibility)

2. What beverages help you feel most satisfied during fasting periods?
   a. Plain water (purist approach)
   b. Sparkling water (adds interest through carbonation)
   c. Tea varieties (different types for different benefits)
   d. Black coffee (potential hunger suppression for many)
   e. Electrolyte-enhanced water (supports mineral balance)

3. Do you experience any negative effects from specific beverages while fasting?
   a. Digestive discomfort (common with coffee on empty stomach for some)
   b. Increased hunger (some find certain beverages stimulate appetite)
   c. Jitteriness or anxiety (caffeine affects some people more during fasted states)
   d. Disrupted sleep if consumed later in day (caffeine sensitivity may increase)

4. What beverages best support your overall fasting consistency and experience?

a. Consider which options make fasting feel sustainable rather than restrictive
   b. Identify what helps manage hunger without technically breaking your fast
   c. Determine which options best support your energy and clarity

5. How does your hydration strategy need to adapt to your activities?
   a. Higher electrolyte needs with exercise or hot weather
   b. Potentially more total fluid during active days
   c. Timing considerations for caffeine based on workout schedule and sleep

Based on your answers, create a personalized hydration plan that supports your fasting practice while honouring your body's unique needs and responses.

David's approach evolved through this kind of reflection: "I discovered that black coffee in the morning helped me extend my fast comfortably, but any coffee after noon disrupted my sleep. So, I switched to green tea in the early afternoon and herbal tea later in the day. I also needed more electrolytes on days I exercised, especially in summer. This personalized approach made fasting feel easy rather than something to endure."

Addressing Emotional Eating With Compassion

Food serves many purposes beyond physical nourishment. For most of us, it's deeply intertwined with comfort, celebration, stress relief, boredom management, and social connection. Intermittent fasting inevitably brings these emotional relationships with food into sharper focus, creating both challenges and opportunities for growth.

Recognizing Emotional Hunger

A powerful benefit of intermittent fasting is the clarity it provides in distinguishing between physical and emotional hunger. With regular practice, you begin to recognize the different sensations and triggers:

Physical hunger typically:
1. Develops gradually over hours
2. Can be satisfied with any nutritious food
3. Subsides after eating a reasonable amount
4. Often manifests as stomach gurgling, empty feeling, or energy decrease

Emotional hunger typically:
1. Arrives suddenly
2. Involves specific cravings for comfort foods or treats
3. Persists despite physical fullness
4. Often connects to specific emotional triggers (stress, boredom, sadness, celebration)

Fasting creates a unique opportunity to observe these patterns because the structure separates you from immediate food access during fasting periods. This separation provides a window to notice impulses without automatically acting on them.

As David observed: "Before intermittent fasting, I never realized how much I ate from boredom or stress. During fasting periods, I'd notice urges to eat when I got stuck on a difficult work problem or felt anxious about a deadline. With eating off the table during those hours, I had to find other ways to address those feelings."

Developing New Emotional Regulation Strategies

When fasting illuminates emotional eating patterns, it creates an opportunity to develop alternative coping mechanisms. Consider these approaches:

1. Practice the pause: When emotional eating urges arise during fasting periods, use the natural boundary of your fasting window to pause and identify what you're really feeling. This simple space between stimulus and response builds emotional intelligence.

2. Expand your emotional vocabulary: Many people have limited language for emotions, defaulting to basic terms like "stressed" or "upset." Learning to distinguish between anxiety, disappointment, loneliness, frustration, or boredom helps address the specific need more effectively.

3. Create a menu of alternative responses: Develop specific strategies for different emotional states. Perhaps physical movement helps with anxiety, creative expression addresses boredom, or social connection alleviates loneliness.

4. Observe without judgment: When emotional eating urges arise, practice noticing them with curiosity rather than criticism. "Interesting—

I want to eat right now even though I know I'm not physically hungry" is more productive than "I have no willpower."

5. **Honor legitimate emotional needs:** Food sometimes provides genuine comfort during difficult times. Rather than viewing all emotional eating as "bad," consider when conscious comfort eating during your eating window might be an appropriate self-care strategy versus when it represents avoidance of addressing deeper needs.

David developed this more balanced perspective: "I realized I'd been using food to manage work stress for years. During my eating window, I now occasionally enjoy a treat mindfully if it's been a particularly challenging day. But more often, I use my fasting periods to identify when I'm reaching for food emotionally and try other approaches first—a quick walk, breathing exercises, or actually addressing the stressful situation directly."

Journal Prompts for Exploring Your Food Relationship

Reflective writing can illuminate emotional eating patterns and create greater awareness. Consider exploring these prompts:

1. What foods do I crave most often? What emotions or situations typically trigger these cravings?
2. When I eat without physical hunger, what needs am I really trying to meet? What alternatives might address those needs more

directly?
3. How did food connect to emotions in my family growing up? What messages did I receive about food's purpose beyond nutrition?
4. When do I feel most at peace with food and eating? What circumstances create a healthy relationship with food for me?
5. How has fasting changed my awareness of my eating patterns? What have I noticed about when and why I want to eat?
6. What non-food activities bring me comfort, joy, or stress relief? How can I incorporate these more intentionally into my life?

This reflection helps transform unconscious patterns into conscious choices. As eating windows become more intentional, the quality of nourishment—both physical and emotional—often naturally improves.

Creating Eating Windows That Feel Abundant

A sustainable intermittent fasting practice depends on eating windows that feel satisfying and abundant rather than deprived or restricted. The goal is to create a healthy relationship with food within your chosen timeframe, not to impose additional limitations that make the practice feel punitive.

Shifting from Scarcity to Sufficiency

Many people initially approach their eating windows with a scarcity mindset—trying to consume as little as possible or feeling guilty about enjoying food. This approach typically backfires, leading to unsatisfying meals, continued food preoccupation, or eventual abandonment of fasting altogether.

Instead, focus on creating eating experiences that feel complete and satisfying. This might include:

1. Prioritizing meal quality over quantity: Rather than rushing through multiple mediocre meals to "fit them in" before your window closes, create one or two thoughtfully prepared, nutritionally complete meals that you eat with full attention.
2. Engaging all senses: Notice colours, aromas, textures, and flavours. Eating with greater sensory awareness increases satisfaction even with moderate portions.
3. Slowing down: Taking time to eat mindfully signals your brain more effectively that you've eaten, increasing satisfaction and improving digestion.
4. Creating meal environments that enhance enjoyment: Something as simple as sitting at a table without screens, using nice dishes, or adding a small bouquet can transform eating from mere consumption to an experience of abundance.
5. Including favourite foods in moderation: Rather than creating additional food rules that make your eating window feel restricted, include reasonable portions of foods you genuinely enjoy alongside nutritious staples.

David found this shift transformative: "I used to try to 'be good' during my eating window, avoiding anything I thought might be 'bad.' This actually left me feeling deprived even though I was eating enough calories. When I shifted to focusing on nutrition while still including small portions of foods I love, fasting became sustainable long-term. I enjoy my meals more now eating twice a day than I did eating five times with constant guilt and restriction."

Planning for Satisfaction

Strategic meal planning helps create eating windows that leave you feeling nourished and content. Consider these approaches:

1. Break your fast with a substantial meal: Ending your fast with a nutritionally complete, satisfying meal sets a positive tone for your eating window and prevents the desperate snacking that can occur when breaking a fast with something insufficient.
2. Consider your hunger patterns: Some people prefer their largest meal earlier in their eating window, while others feel more satisfied ending with their main meal. Experiment to find your optimal pattern.
3. Include all macronutrients: Meals containing adequate protein, healthy fats, and appropriate carbohydrates for your activity level provide longer-lasting satisfaction than meals heavily skewed toward one macronutrient.
4. Embrace volume from fibre-rich foods: Vegetables, fruits, legumes, and whole grains add satisfying volume and nutrition without excessive calories, helping meals feel

abundant.
5. Find your satisfaction signals: Learn to recognize when you're comfortably satisfied rather than eating until uncomfortably full or stopping before genuine satisfaction.

David's strategy evolved through experimentation: "I found I feel best with two main meals—the first around noon with plenty of protein and vegetables, and the second about six hours later with more carbohydrates. This pattern gives me stable energy throughout my eating window and helps me sleep better at night."

Implementation Checklist: Optimizing Your Nutrition During Eating Windows

Use this checklist to enhance your eating experience and support your fasting practice:

1. Assess your current fast-breaking meals and note how they affect your energy, satisfaction, and subsequent hunger.
2. Create a list of 3-5 satisfying meal options for breaking your fast that include protein, healthy fats, and fibre.
3. Evaluate your hydration strategy during fasting periods and identify improvements if needed.
4. Experiment with electrolyte supplementation if you experience headaches, dizziness, or fatigue during fasting.
5. Track your emotional eating triggers for one week, noting when non-hunger eating urges arise and what emotions precede them.
6. Develop two non-food strategies for each of

your common emotional triggers.
7. Identify one way to enhance your eating environment to support mindfulness and enjoyment.
8. Plan balanced meals that fit your eating window and leave you feeling satisfied.
9. Experiment with meal timing and composition within your eating window to find your optimal pattern.
10. Create a simple system for ensuring nutritional completeness when eating fewer meals.
11. Review your fasting beverage options and select those that best support your goals and preferences.
12. Schedule a weekly review of how your nutrition strategy is supporting your overall fasting experience.

The relationship between what you eat during your eating windows and how you feel during fasting periods is deeply interconnected. By approaching both with intention and awareness, you create a harmonious cycle—nutritious, satisfying meals support comfortable fasting periods, which in turn enhance your appreciation and enjoyment of food.

In our next chapter, we'll explore how to overcome common challenges and truly make fasting your own—adapting the practice to your unique lifestyle, schedule, and preferences. You'll learn strategies for handling social situations, managing energy fluctuations, and personalizing your approach for sustainable success.

Remember that the goal isn't perfection but progress

—gradually refining your approach based on your body's wisdom and feedback. With each fasting cycle, you're developing greater metabolic flexibility, food awareness, and body intuition that will serve you well beyond the specifics of any fasting protocol.

CHAPTER 4: OVERCOMING CHALLENGES AND MAKING FASTING YOUR OWN

The Universal Nature of Challenges

If you've encountered obstacles in your fasting journey, I want you to know something important: you're not alone, and you're not doing anything wrong. Every single person who has successfully integrated intermittent fasting into their life has faced challenges along the way. These hurdles aren't signs of failure—they're natural parts of the adaptation process and opportunities to deepen your practice.

What separates those who make fasting a sustainable part of their lives from those who abandon it isn't an absence of challenges. Rather, it's the development of specific skills to navigate these challenges with flexibility, self-awareness, and practical strategies. In this chapter, we'll build that exact skillset.

The most common challenges fall into several categories: physical sensations like hunger and energy fluctuations; interpersonal issues like social pressure and family dynamics; and practical concerns like adapting fasting to complex schedules or special circumstances. We'll address each of these areas with both emotional wisdom and tactical approaches, transforming potential roadblocks into stepping stones on your journey.

Remember that overcoming these challenges doesn't just make fasting possible—it makes the practice yours. Each obstacle you navigate successfully personalizes your approach and builds your confidence as the true expert on your unique body and needs. This chapter isn't just about problem-solving; it's about empowerment through personalization.

Hunger: From Emergency to Information

Perhaps no sensation is more central to the fasting experience than hunger. For many beginners, hunger feels urgent, uncomfortable, even anxiety-producing—an emergency that requires immediate resolution. Yet experienced practitioners describe a transformed relationship with this sensation, where hunger becomes interesting information rather than an alarm requiring immediate action.

Understanding hunger's true nature can revolutionize your fasting experience. Most people don't realize that hunger follows a wave-like pattern rather than a continuous intensification. Hunger typically rises, peaks, and then—if not responded to with food—naturally subsides as your body adapts by accessing stored energy. Many beginners never discover this pattern because they respond to the rising edge of hunger immediately, never experiencing how it naturally recedes.

This transformation is exactly what Karen, a 52-

year-old teacher, discovered after struggling with her initial fasting attempts. "I thought there was something wrong with me because hunger felt so intense and uncomfortable," she explained. "But when I finally stayed with it instead of immediately eating, I discovered something remarkable—after about 20 minutes, the urgent feeling would pass, and I'd feel fine for hours. That knowledge completely changed my relationship with hunger. I stopped fearing it."

The Three Dimensions of Hunger

To work more skilfully with hunger, it helps to understand its different dimensions:

Physical hunger involves actual bodily sensations—perhaps an empty feeling in your stomach, light gurgling sounds, or a certain hollow sensation. These physical manifestations are rarely as severe or dangerous as we imagine them to be. With practice, you can observe these sensations with curiosity rather than resistance.

Emotional hunger includes the feelings that arise around hunger—perhaps anxiety, irritability, or a sense of deprivation. These emotional responses are often conditioned by past experiences and beliefs about hunger rather than the physical sensations themselves. Recognizing the difference between the physical sensation and your emotional reaction to it creates space for new responses.

Mental hunger encompasses thoughts about hunger—"I can't handle this," "This is too hard," or "I need to eat right now." These thoughts often catastrophize normal hunger sensations, making them seem more threatening or permanent than they actually are. With awareness, you can recognize these as habitual thoughts rather than objective reality.

By distinguishing between these dimensions, you gain the ability to work with each aspect separately. You might notice physical hunger sensations while choosing different emotional responses and more supportive thoughts.

Try This Now: The Hunger Wave Exploration

This exercise builds your capacity to experience hunger with greater equanimity:

1. The next time you feel hungry during a fasting period, commit to staying with the sensation for 20 minutes before deciding whether to break your fast.
2. Find a comfortable position and take three deep breaths.
3. Notice where you feel hunger in your body. Is it in your stomach? Throat? Elsewhere? What are the specific sensations—empty, hollow, tight, gurgling?
4. Rate the intensity of the physical sensation on a scale of 1-10.
5. Notice any emotions connected to the hunger. Anxiety? Irritation? Worry? Simply acknowledge these feelings without judgment.
6. Observe any thoughts about the hunger. Are you telling yourself stories about what will happen if you don't eat immediately?
7. For the next 20 minutes, engage in

a moderately distracting activity—perhaps work, reading, or light physical activity. Drink a glass of water with a pinch of salt.
8. After 20 minutes, check in again with the hunger sensation. Rate its intensity again on the same 1-10 scale. Has it changed? Many people are surprised to discover the intensity has decreased significantly.
9. Whatever you discover, acknowledge it with curiosity rather than judgment. You're gathering valuable data about your body's patterns.

With repeated practice, this exercise builds your "hunger muscle"—your capacity to experience hunger without immediate reactivity. This skill transforms fasting from a test of willpower into a practice of awareness and choice.

Practical Strategies for Hunger Management

Beyond building general hunger tolerance, specific tactical approaches can help manage hunger sensations during fasting periods:

Hydration: Thirst sometimes masquerades as hunger. Staying well-hydrated throughout your fasting window can reduce hunger sensations. Add electrolytes (particularly sodium) for enhanced effectiveness.

Strategic distraction: Engaging in activities that capture your attention can help hunger waves pass more easily. Many find that hunger is most noticeable during idle moments and less apparent when meaningfully engaged.

Caffeine timing: For those who tolerate it well, caffeine can blunt hunger sensations temporarily. Black coffee or tea strategically timed around your typical hunger peaks can help smooth the fasting experience.

Hunger pattern identification: Track when hunger typically peaks for you during fasting periods. Scheduling engaging activities, meetings, or workouts during these times can make them easier to navigate.

Environment management: Visual food cues can trigger hunger even when physiological hunger is absent. Creating distance from food environments during fasting periods—like avoiding the kitchen or food-centred activities—can reduce unnecessary hunger triggers.

Reframing language: Simple language shifts can change your experience. Try replacing "I'm starving" with "I'm experiencing hunger sensations" or "I'm fasting now" instead of "I can't eat." These subtle changes reduce hunger's dramatic emotional charge.

Mindful self-talk: When hunger arises, remind yourself: "This is a normal sensation that will pass" or "My body is accessing stored energy right now, which is exactly what I want."

Karen found that a combination of approaches worked best for her: "I discovered that my hunger peaked around 10 am, so I started scheduling my most engaging classes during that time. I also kept a water bottle with lemon and salt nearby. But the biggest difference came from simply reminding myself that hunger comes in waves that pass naturally.

That knowledge alone made the sensation much less threatening."

Energy Fluctuations: Working With Your Natural Rhythms

Another common challenge involves navigating energy changes during fasting. Many beginners expect consistent energy throughout their days, but our bodies naturally experience energy fluctuations regardless of eating patterns. Fasting can initially amplify these fluctuations before ultimately helping to stabilize them.

Understanding your unique energy patterns helps you work with rather than against your body's natural rhythms. This awareness allows you to schedule activities appropriately and make adjustments that support steady, sustainable energy throughout your day.

Mapping Your Energy Patterns

Begin by tracking your energy levels throughout the day for about a week using a simple 1-10 scale. Note times when you feel most energetic and focused versus periods of lower energy or mental fog. Look for patterns:

1. Do you naturally feel more energetic in the morning or evening?
2. How does your energy typically flow throughout the day?
3. When do you experience your sharpest mental clarity?

4. How do fasting periods affect these patterns?
5. Do certain activities or foods noticeably impact your energy?

This energy mapping reveals your body's natural circadian rhythms and helps you identify how fasting interacts with these patterns. Rather than fighting your natural energy flows, you can align your fasting approach with them.

Consider Rachel, a 45-year-old graphic designer who initially struggled with afternoon energy crashes during fasting. "I started with a 16:8 schedule, eating from 8am to 4pm because that's what I read was best. But I was consistently hitting an energy wall around 3pm, which was disastrous for my work."

By tracking her energy patterns, Rachel made an important discovery: "I realized I naturally have more energy in the late afternoon and evening. When I shifted my eating window to noon-8pm instead, everything changed. My mornings became incredibly productive fasting periods with great mental clarity, and I was eating during my natural energy dips, which helped smooth them out."

Adapting to the Metabolic Transition

A specific energy challenge many beginners face occurs during the metabolic transition from using primarily glucose for fuel to accessing fat stores—sometimes called "hitting the wall" or "the switch." This transition typically happens 12-16 hours into a fast, when liver glycogen becomes depleted.

During early fasting attempts, this transition might feel uncomfortable—perhaps a period of lower energy, slight dizziness, or mental fog. However, as your metabolic flexibility improves with consistent practice, this transition becomes smoother and eventually nearly imperceptible.

Short-term strategies to navigate this transition include:

Electrolyte support: Adding a pinch of high-quality salt to water can often alleviate symptoms rapidly.

Movement: Light physical activity like a brief walk can help stimulate circulation and metabolic transition.

Patience: Recognizing that this phase is temporary and typically passes within 30-60 minutes can help you wait it out with less frustration.

Long-term improvement comes through consistency. Each time you move through this metabolic transition, your body becomes more efficient at it. Many practitioners report that after 2-3 weeks of consistent fasting, the transition becomes barely noticeable or even brings a welcomed energy boost.

Try This Now: Energy Navigation Micro-Experiment

This simple experiment helps you discover how different activities affect your energy during fasting:

1. The next time you experience an energy dip while fasting, rate your energy level on a scale of 1-10 before doing anything.
2. Choose ONE of these interventions to try:

    a. Drink 12-16 oz of water with a pinch of salt
    b. Take a 5-minute brisk walk
    c. Perform 20 jumping jacks or similar brief exercise
    d. Step outside for fresh air and sunlight for 5 minutes
    e. Practice 2 minutes of deep breathing
3. After completing your chosen intervention, wait 10 minutes and then rate your energy level again on the same 1-10 scale.
4. On subsequent days, try different interventions from the list during energy dips.
5. Compare the effectiveness of different approaches for your unique body.

This experiment builds your personal toolkit for energy management. Rachel discovered her most effective strategy: "A short walk followed by water with salt works like magic for me during afternoon energy dips. It's simple but makes a huge difference in how I feel."

Social Situations: Navigating the Interpersonal Landscape

Perhaps no aspect of intermittent fasting creates more anxiety for beginners than navigating social situations. Food is deeply woven into our social fabric —we connect over meals, celebrate with feasts, and express care through cooking for others. Changing your eating patterns inevitably affects these interactions, but with thoughtful approaches, social situations can be navigated gracefully.

Family Meals and Household Dynamics

When you live with others, your fasting practice affects not just you but household routines as well. Clear, non-defensive communication becomes essential. Here are approaches that have helped many practitioners:

Focus on timing rather than restriction: Frame your practice as changing when you eat rather than restricting what you eat. This perspective feels less judgmental to others who might otherwise think their food choices are being criticized.

Maintain connection rituals: If family meals have been important connection points, find ways to preserve the social aspect even when not eating. Perhaps sit with family during their breakfast even if you're fasting, focusing on conversation rather than food.

Be flexible for special occasions: Sustainable fasting adapts around important family events rather than creating rigid restrictions that generate resentment.

Involve family in decisions: When your fasting affects meal timing for others, include them in planning conversations rather than unilaterally changing routines.

Respect others' choices: Just as you want your fasting practice respected, extend the same courtesy to others' eating choices without evangelizing.

For Rachel, family dinner presented her biggest challenge: "My husband and teenage kids were used to me preparing dinner around 6:30pm. Even though I had shifted my eating window to end earlier, I didn't want to disrupt this important family time."

Her solution honoured both her needs and family connection: "I still prepared and sat down for dinner with everyone. I just had a cup of herbal tea while they ate, focusing on the conversation instead of the food. On weekends, I'd shift my eating window later so I could fully participate in family dinners. This flexibility preserved what mattered most—our time together—while still maintaining my fasting practice most days."

Social Gatherings and Dining Out

Broader social situations present different challenges. Here are strategies for navigating them with confidence:

Plan around important events: When possible, adjust your fasting schedule to accommodate special social meals. Intermittent fasting should enhance your life, not isolate you from meaningful connections.

Have simple explanations ready: Prepare brief, neutral responses for when people notice you're not eating, such as "I've found I feel better when I eat during a specific window of time" or "I'm giving my digestive system a rest until later today."

Shift attention from food to connection: Remember that the primary purpose of social gatherings is human connection. Actively engaging in conversation helps both you and others focus less on whether you're eating.

Choose restaurants strategically: When dining out during your eating window, suggest places with options that support your health goals. When socializing during fasting hours, venues with engaging activities beyond just eating can shift the focus.

Practice confident body language: Your comfort with your choices influences how others respond. Explain your choices matter-of-factly without apology or excessive justification.

Rachel found these approaches transformed potentially awkward situations: "I used to dread client lunches when I was fasting. Now I simply order sparkling water with lime and say, 'I'm trying a new eating schedule that's working really well for my energy.' Then I immediately ask them a question about their business. People are generally far more interested in talking about themselves than what I'm eating or not eating."

Sample Scripts for Common Scenarios

Having prepared responses reduces anxiety in social situations. These examples can be adapted to your personal style:

For declining food: "Thanks so much for offering. Everything looks delicious, but I'm not eating until later today. I'd love the recipe though!"

For explaining briefly: "I practice intermittent fasting, which means I eat during a specific window of time each day. It's been great for my energy and focus."

For deflecting food pressure: "I appreciate your concern, but this eating pattern really works well for me. I'd love to hear more about your project instead..."

For family members: "This isn't about not enjoying your

cooking—it's about finding an eating pattern that helps me feel my best. I'd still love to sit with you during meals for the company."

For hosting others: "Please go ahead and enjoy! Just because I'm not eating right now doesn't mean you shouldn't. I'm happy just being together."

The key with all these responses is delivering them with comfortable confidence rather than apologetic uncertainty. Your eating patterns are a personal health choice that doesn't require defence or justification.

Adapting Fasting to Different Lifestyles

One of intermittent fasting's greatest strengths is its flexibility—it can be adapted to various life circumstances rather than requiring your life to conform to a rigid protocol. Let's explore how to customize fasting for different lifestyle situations.

Shift Work and Irregular Schedules

Shift workers face unique challenges with fasting since their activity and sleep patterns may not align with conventional circadian rhythms. However, intermittent fasting can still provide benefits with thoughtful adaptation:

Anchor to your sleep cycle, not the clock: Rather than focusing on specific times of day, structure your fasting periods in relation to when you sleep. For example, if you work overnight, your eating window might be the first 8 hours after waking, regardless of what time that is.

Maintain consistency within rotation periods: If you work rotating shifts, try to maintain a consistent fasting pattern during each rotation period rather than changing daily.

Prioritize quality nutrition during work shifts: When your work schedule requires eating at unusual times, focus on nutritionally dense, balanced meals that support sustained energy.

Use fasting to aid shift transitions: Some find that fasting periods can actually help reset their body clock when transitioning between different shift schedules.

James, a 34-year-old emergency room nurse working rotating 12-hour shifts, found intermittent fasting surprisingly adaptable: "I initially thought fasting would be impossible with my schedule. Then I realized I could focus on the pattern rather than specific clock times. I aim for a 16-hour fast followed by an 8-hour eating window, but the timing shifts based on my work schedule. During night shifts, I'll eat when I wake up in the afternoon and during my first few hours at work. On day shifts, I'll eat from midday until evening."

Parenting and Family Responsibilities

Parents of young children face different challenges—unpredictable schedules, the need to prepare food for others while fasting, and modelling healthy behaviours. Consider these approaches:

Capitalize on natural fasting periods: Many parents find that the evening after children's bedtime until late morning works well for fasting, as it often corresponds with their lowest energy demands.

Build a self-care mindset: Framing fasting as part of your self-care routine—like sleep or exercise—helps prioritize it without guilt amid family responsibilities.

Involve age-appropriate education: For older children, age-appropriate explanations about different hunger patterns and eating schedules can normalize your practice while teaching flexible approaches to health.

Prepare food mindfully: When preparing food for others while fasting, use it as an opportunity for mindfulness practice rather than torture. Focus on the sensory experience of cooking and the care you're providing rather than the desire to eat.

Remain flexible for family harmony: Adapt your fasting schedule for important family meals and celebrations, remembering that sustainability comes through balance, not rigidity.

Lisa, a mother of three young children, shared her approach: "I fast from after dinner until lunch the next day, which gives me about 16-18 hours. This works because I'm busy with morning routines when hunger might otherwise be challenging, and I can still have dinner with my family. During weekend family brunches, I adjust my schedule because those meals are important for our family connection."

Travel and Inconsistent Environments

Travel presents unique fasting challenges due to changing time zones, irregular schedules, and different food availability. Yet many find fasting particularly beneficial while traveling to maintain energy and reduce jet lag:

Use fasting to reset circadian rhythms: Extended fasts (with proper hydration) during travel can actually help combat jet lag by allowing your body to more quickly adapt to new time zones.

Pack fasting-friendly options: Traveling with electrolyte supplements, herbal teas, and perhaps emergency protein options helps you maintain your practice in unpredictable environments.

Adapt to local cultural patterns: In some situations, adjusting your fasting schedule to accommodate local customs and meal times shows cultural respect while still maintaining some fasting benefits.

Focus on window quality over duration: During particularly challenging travel periods, you might shorten your fasting window but increase your focus on high-quality nutrition during eating periods.

Use fasting to navigate limited food options: When healthy food choices are scarce, fasting periods can reduce the total exposure to less-optimal options while allowing you to enjoy the most worthwhile local cuisine during eating windows.

James found fasting particularly valuable during work travel: "I used to struggle with terrible eating during conferences—conference centre food, late dinners, and airport meals were a digestive nightmare. Now I typically fast through breakfast, enjoy a good lunch and dinner, and feel so much better. The structure actually gives me more freedom to enjoy good meals without feeling terrible."

High-Stress Periods and Special Circumstances

During especially demanding life periods—perhaps significant work projects, family challenges, or other stressors—fasting approaches may need temporary modification:

Consider shorter fasting windows: During high-stress periods, moderating to 12-14 hour fasts rather than 16-20 hours might better support your body's stress response.

Increase focus on nutrition quality: Stress increases nutrient needs, making food quality during eating windows even more important during challenging times.

Add stress-management practices: Combining stress-reduction techniques with modified fasting often yields better results than either approach alone.

Return to your baseline gradually: After the stressful period passes, gradually return to your usual fasting pattern rather than immediately resuming more challenging protocols.

Honor unique physical demands: Special circumstances like illness, recovery, or unusual physical demands may require temporary breaks from fasting or significant modifications to support your body's needs.

Rachel navigated a particularly demanding work project with this flexible mindset: "During a month-long intensive project with 60-hour work weeks, I scaled back from 16:8 to 12:12 fasting. I knew my body needed more support during that time. Once the project ended, I spent two weeks at 14:10 before returning to my usual 16:8 pattern. This flexibility prevented me from abandoning fasting altogether during stress."

Decision Point: Personalizing Your Fasting Approach

After experimenting with basic fasting protocols, you reach an important decision point: how to personalize your approach for optimal results and sustainability. Consider these questions to guide your personalization process:

1. When during the day do you experience your greatest natural energy and mental clarity?
    a. Early morning (suggests fasting later in the day)
    b. Midday (suggests possible midday eating window)
    c. Evening (suggests eating earlier in the day)
    d. Variable (suggests flexible approach based on daily patterns)
2. Which fasting window duration leaves you feeling energized rather than depleted?
    a. 12 hours (gentler approach, often good for high-stress periods or beginners)
    b. 14-16 hours (moderate approach balancing benefits and sustainability)
    c. 16-20 hours (more advanced approach for those well-adapted)
    d. Variable based on activity and needs (flexible approach)

3. What eating window timing best accommodates your non-negotiable social and family priorities?
    a. Morning into afternoon eating
    b. Midday into evening eating
    c. Afternoon into night eating
    d. Variable based on social schedule

4. How does your fasting pattern need to accommodate your work schedule and responsibilities?
    a. Regular workday schedule
    b. Shift work or rotating schedule
    c. Frequent travel
    d. Variable professional demands

5. What approach to consistency works best for your personality and lifestyle?
    a. Same schedule every day (best for those who thrive on routine)
    b. Weekday/weekend variation (balances structure with flexibility)
    c. Fully flexible based on daily needs (best for unpredictable lifestyles)
    d. Cyclical approaches (varying fasting approaches based on monthly patterns)

Your answers to these questions help create your personalized fasting framework—not a rigid protocol, but a flexible structure that honours your unique body, lifestyle, and preferences.

Rachel's personalization process illustrates this

approach: "After experimenting for several months, I found that a 16:8 pattern works best for me, eating between noon and 8pm on weekdays. This gives me focused morning work time during my natural mental clarity peak. On weekends, I shift to a 14:10 pattern with an earlier eating window starting around 10am to enjoy brunch with friends and family. During my menstrual cycle, I ease back to 12:12 for a few days when my body needs more support. This personalized approach means I maintain my practice consistently rather than swinging between perfect adherence and complete abandonment."

Recognizing Your Personal Patterns

Sustained success with intermittent fasting comes through developing awareness of your unique patterns and responses. This self-knowledge allows you to make informed adjustments rather than following generic guidelines that might not serve your specific body.

Body Awareness Development

The regular alternation between fasted and fed states creates an excellent laboratory for developing deeper body awareness. Over time, you'll likely notice patterns in:

Hunger fluctuations: When hunger naturally peaks and subsides during your day.
Energy rhythms: Your natural energy highs and lows, and how fasting affects them.
Mental clarity patterns: Times when your thinking feels sharpest versus foggier.
Mood correlations: How your emotional state relates to

fasting and eating.

Physical sensations: Digestive comfort, physical energy, and other bodily sensations.

Sleep quality: How different fasting patterns affect your rest.

This growing body awareness becomes invaluable not just for fasting but for overall health self-management. Many practitioners report that the increased sensitivity to their body's signals transfers to other areas—better hydration awareness, more intuitive exercise choices, and improved stress recognition.

James described this evolution: "Before fasting, I barely noticed my body's signals until they became extremely demanding. Now I can detect subtle shifts in my energy, hunger, and focus. This awareness helps me make small adjustments before problems become significant—not just with eating but with rest, stress management, and physical activity."

Pattern Recognition Tools

Several approaches can accelerate your pattern recognition:

Simple tracking: Briefly noting hunger levels, energy, mental clarity, and mood at set intervals helps identify patterns that might otherwise go unnoticed.

Experiment and observe: Intentionally varying your fasting approach (longer or shorter windows, different timing) and observing the effects builds your understanding of your unique responses.

Body scan practice: Taking 2-3 minutes several times

daily to mentally scan through your body develops greater sensitivity to physical sensations.

Reflection questions: Regularly asking yourself questions like "When did I feel most energetic today?" or "How did my hunger fluctuate?" draws attention to patterns you might otherwise miss.

Rachel found tracking particularly valuable: "I noticed that if I broke my fast with a carb-heavy meal, I'd have an energy crash 90 minutes later. But if I broke it with a balanced meal including protein and healthy fats, my energy remained stable for hours. I would never have connected these patterns without simple tracking."

Try This Now: Personal Pattern Detection

This three-day awareness exercise helps you identify your unique patterns:

1. Select three consecutive typical days (not holidays or unusual circumstances).
2. Set an alarm to check in with your body every two hours during waking hours.
3. At each check-in, quickly note:
    a. Hunger level (1-10 scale)
    b. Energy level (1-10 scale)
    c. Mental clarity (1-10 scale)
    d. Predominant mood or emotion
    e. Last time you ate or drank anything besides water
    f. Any other notable physical sensations
4. After three days, review your notes looking for patterns:
    a. When does hunger typically peak?

      b. When is your energy naturally highest? Lowest?

      c. How long after eating do you notice energy or clarity changes?

      d. Are there consistent patterns to your mood fluctuations?

5. Consider how you might adjust your fasting practice to work with these natural patterns rather than against them.

This simple exercise often reveals surprising patterns that can inform more effective fasting timing. Lisa discovered through this practice that her mental clarity peaked about 14-16 hours into her fast: "I realized I could schedule my most demanding work tasks during this natural clarity window, taking advantage of this heightened cognitive state rather than fighting through mental fog at other times."

Becoming Your Own Fasting Expert

The ultimate goal of this chapter isn't just helping you overcome challenges—it's empowering you to become your own fasting expert. While research and guidelines provide useful frameworks, your body's unique responses represent the most important data for your personal practice.

The Evolution of Fasting Mastery

As you continue your fasting journey, your practice typically evolves through several stages:

      1. Protocol Following: Initially, you follow established approaches exactly as described,

seeking external guidance and validation.
2. Pattern Recognition: With experience, you begin noticing your unique responses and making minor adjustments based on personal feedback.
3. Principle Application: Eventually, you understand the underlying principles well enough to modify approaches confidently while maintaining core benefits.
4. Intuitive Practice: At its most evolved stage, fasting becomes an intuitive practice guided by body wisdom and deep personal experience rather than external rules.

This evolution doesn't happen overnight, but with consistent practice and thoughtful attention, you develop increasing confidence in your ability to adapt fasting to your unique needs. The challenges you overcome become the very experiences that build your expertise.

James reflected on this evolution after 18 months of practice: "When I started, I was rigidly following the 16:8 protocol regardless of how I felt or what was happening in my life. Now my practice looks different almost every day, yet paradoxically more consistent because it's sustainable. Some days I fast 18 hours when it feels right; other days 14 hours when my body needs more support. The difference is I'm making these adjustments based on my body's signals and my life's demands rather than arbitrary rules."

Iterative Refinement Process

Becoming your own fasting expert involves continuous

refinement through a simple process:

1. Observe: Notice your body's responses without judgment
2. Reflect: Consider patterns and potential adjustments
3. Experiment: Make small, intentional changes
4. Evaluate: Assess the results of your experiments
5. Integrate: Incorporate successful adjustments into your practice

This iterative process transforms challenges from frustrating obstacles into valuable data points that inform your evolving practice. Each adjustment becomes an opportunity to deepen your body wisdom and self-trust.

Rachel described her iterative approach: "When I noticed afternoon headaches during fasting, I first experimented with electrolytes, which helped significantly. Then I noticed the headaches were worse on days I had less sleep, so I adjusted to shorter fasts following poor sleep nights. Each challenge led to a refinement that made my practice more sustainable."

Trust Your Body's Wisdom

Perhaps the most important aspect of becoming your own fasting expert is developing trust in your body's innate wisdom. While this may sound abstract, it manifests in very practical ways:

Recognizing genuine needs versus habitual patterns: Developing the discernment to distinguish between true body requirements and conditioned habits

Honouring unique responses: Accepting that your optimal approach might differ from others based on your specific physiology and circumstances

Balanced flexibility: Finding the middle path between rigid adherence to protocols and complete abandonment of structure

Compassionate adaptation: Making adjustments with self-care rather than self-criticism when circumstances require modification

Lisa's journey exemplifies this growing body trust: "The biggest change wasn't in my fasting schedule but in my relationship with my body. I've developed confidence in my ability to hear and respond to my body's signals. Sometimes that means extending a fast when I'm feeling great; other times it means breaking a fast early when my body needs support. This trust feels like the most valuable outcome of my fasting practice."

Personalization Checklist: Adapting Fasting to Your Life

Use this checklist to ensure your fasting practice truly fits your unique body and lifestyle:

1. Identify your natural energy patterns and align your fasting windows to work with rather than against these rhythms.
2. Determine your optimal fasting duration based on how you feel during and after different length fasts.
3. Create strategies for your specific hunger challenge times based on when you typically

experience strongest hunger sensations.
4. Develop approaches for common social situations in your life, including family meals, work functions, and social gatherings.
5. Adjust your fasting schedule to accommodate non-negotiable aspects of your lifestyle and relationships.
6. Plan modifications for special circumstances like travel, high-stress periods, or unusual physical demands.
7. Experiment with different fast-breaking meals to identify what works best for your unique body.
8. Create simple tracking systems that help you recognize patterns in your energy, hunger, and wellbeing.
9. Build a repertoire of responses for common fasting challenges specific to your life circumstances.
10. Schedule regular practice reviews to assess what's working well and what might benefit from adjustment.
11. Develop a flexible framework rather than rigid rules—guidelines that can adapt to changing circumstances while maintaining core benefits.
12. Establish communication approaches for explaining your choices to important people in your life.
13. Create environmental supports that make your personalized approach easier to maintain.
14. Identify your non-negotiable self-care

practices that support your fasting experience.
15. Recognize signs that indicate when to modify your approach temporarily based on your body's changing needs.

Your personalized approach might look quite different from how you started or from what others practice—and that's exactly as it should be. The most successful fasting practice isn't the one that follows a particular protocol perfectly; it's the one that you can maintain consistently because it truly works with your unique body and life.

As you continue developing your personalized practice, remember that challenges aren't failures—they're valuable feedback that guides your evolution. Each obstacle you navigate successfully adds to your body wisdom and self-trust, transforming intermittent fasting from something you follow externally to something that flows naturally from within.

In our next chapter, we'll explore special considerations for women's hormonal health, physical activity, and exercise—areas where thoughtful personalization becomes particularly important for optimal results and wellbeing.

CHAPTER 5: SPECIAL CONSIDERATIONS: WOMEN'S HEALTH, ACTIVITY, AND EXERCISE

The Complex Intersection of Gender, Body, and Food

When it comes to intermittent fasting, we need to acknowledge an important truth: biological differences matter, particularly when it comes to hormonal health. Women's bodies respond differently to fasting than men's bodies do—not better or worse, but distinctly. This isn't just about reproductive health; it's about the intricate hormonal symphony that influences energy, mood, metabolism, and overall wellbeing throughout a woman's life.

These differences aren't always addressed in mainstream fasting literature, which often bases recommendations on research conducted primarily on male subjects. This oversight isn't just a matter of inclusion—it can lead to frustrating experiences when women follow approaches that don't honour their unique physiology.

At the same time, the relationship between women,

food, and body image in our culture is often fraught with judgment, pressure, and unrealistic expectations. Many women approach any change in eating patterns carrying the weight of previous diet experiences, body dissatisfaction, or complex emotional relationships with food.

In this chapter, we'll explore these important considerations with both scientific accuracy and emotional sensitivity. My aim is to create a space where women's experiences are validated, their unique physiology is respected, and practical approaches are provided that support hormonal health rather than disrupting it.

For all readers—regardless of gender—this chapter offers valuable insights into creating a more balanced relationship with movement and exercise while fasting. We'll explore how to approach physical activity in ways that complement your fasting practice rather than undermining it, with emphasis on joyful movement that sustains energy rather than depletes it.

Important Medical Considerations

Before we delve deeper, I must emphasize that the information in this chapter, while evidence-based, cannot replace personalized medical advice. This is particularly important when discussing hormonal health and significant changes to diet and exercise patterns.

If you have any existing medical conditions—especially those affecting hormonal balance, reproductive health, or metabolism—please consult with your healthcare provider before implementing intermittent fasting. This includes conditions such as:

1. Polycystic Ovary Syndrome (PCOS)
2. Endometriosis
3. Thyroid disorders
4. History of amenorrhea (absence of menstruation)
5. Fertility concerns
6. Pregnancy or breastfeeding (periods when fasting is generally not recommended)
7. History of disordered eating or eating disorders
8. Diabetes or insulin resistance
9. Adrenal dysfunction

Even if you don't have diagnosed conditions, significant changes to your cycle, unusual symptoms, or persistent discomfort during fasting warrant professional medical attention. Your body's signals deserve respect and appropriate care.

Throughout this chapter, I'll provide guidance based on current research and clinical experience, but please view these as starting points for conversation with your healthcare provider rather than definitive prescriptions for your unique situation.

Women's Hormonal Considerations

Women's bodies have evolved sophisticated hormonal systems that respond quickly to environmental signals, including energy availability. This sensitivity served an important evolutionary purpose—protecting reproductive capacity during times of food scarcity.

While this adaptation was valuable for survival, it means that women's bodies may respond to fasting differently than men's bodies do.

The Menstrual Cycle and Fasting

For women of reproductive age, the menstrual cycle creates a monthly rhythm of hormonal fluctuations that affect everything from energy and mood to metabolism and hunger. Understanding these natural fluctuations can help you adapt your fasting practice to work with your body rather than against it.

A typical 28-day cycle (though individual cycles vary considerably) includes these phases:

Follicular Phase (approximately days 1-14, beginning with menstruation) During this phase, estrogen gradually rises while progesterone remains low. Many women find they naturally tolerate fasting better during this phase due to improved insulin sensitivity and often more stable energy and mood. This can be an ideal time to practice your standard fasting approach or even slightly extend fasting windows if your body responds well.

Ovulation (approximately day 14) This brief phase marks the release of an egg and a surge of hormones. Some women notice increased energy and appetite during this time. Maintaining your regular fasting practice is generally well-tolerated, though you might notice slightly increased hunger.

Luteal Phase (approximately days 15-28) During this pre-menstrual phase, progesterone rises and then both estrogen and progesterone fall if pregnancy doesn't occur. This phase often brings increased insulin resistance, higher caloric needs (up to 250-350 additional calories daily for some women), and sometimes more intense hunger or cravings. Many women benefit from modifying their fasting practice during this phase—perhaps shortening fasting windows or practicing a more gentle approach.

Menstruation (approximately days 1-5) As your cycle begins again, hormone levels reach their lowest point. Individual responses vary widely—some women find fasting quite comfortable during this time, while others need more nourishment and gentler approaches.

Visual Reference: Fasting Adaptations Across the Menstrual Cycle

Imagine a circular calendar representing the typical menstrual cycle, with these suggested adaptations:

Follicular Phase (Days 1-14)

1. Standard fasting practice typically well-tolerated
2. Potential for slightly longer fasting windows if desired
3. Focus on rebuilding iron stores with nutrient-dense foods during eating windows
4. Often a good time for more intense workouts during fasted states

Ovulation (Around Day 14)
1. Maintain standard fasting approach
2. May need slightly more protein and healthy fats

3. Energy usually supports standard exercise intensity

Early Luteal Phase (Days 15-21)
   1. Consider standard to moderate fasting windows
   2. Emphasis on adequate protein and fibre to manage increasing hunger
   3. May benefit from carbohydrates with evening meals
   4. Moderate exercise intensity usually well-tolerated

Late Luteal Phase (Days 22-28)
   1. Consider shortening fasting windows by 2-4 hours
   2. Increase emphasis on nutrient density during eating windows
   3. Particularly important to include carbohydrates with meals
   4. Gentler exercise may be preferable
   5. Extra attention to sleep quality and stress management

Menstruation (Days 1-5)
   1. Personalized approach based on how you feel
   2. Focus on iron-rich foods and hydration
   3. Listen closely to your body regarding both fasting and exercise intensity

Practical Application for Cycle Awareness

Rather than viewing these cyclical changes as limitations, consider them opportunities to practice body awareness and develop a more intuitive approach to fasting. Here's how to implement cycle-sensitive fasting:

1. Track your cycle: Use a journal or app to track your cycle length, symptoms, energy levels, and hunger patterns for at least 2-3 months. This personal data is far more valuable than generic guidelines.
2. Identify your personal patterns: Notice when during your cycle you naturally feel more or less hungry, have higher or lower energy, or experience mood changes that might affect your fasting experience.
3. Create a flexible framework: Rather than one rigid fasting schedule, develop 2-3 different approaches you can rotate through based on your cycle phase:
    a. Standard approach (perhaps 16:8 or your preferred window)
    b. Modified approach with shorter fasting periods (perhaps 12-14 hours)
    c. Occasionally, a more advanced approach during your highest energy phases if appropriate
4. Emphasize cycle-supportive nutrition: During eating windows, focus on foods that support hormonal balance for your specific phase:
    a. Follicular phase: Lighter proteins, fresh fruits and vegetables, fermented foods
    b. Ovulatory phase: Antioxidant-rich foods, healthy fats, raw vegetables
    c. Luteal phase: Complex carbohydrates,

magnesium-rich foods, warming cooked meals
   d. Menstrual phase: Iron-rich foods, anti-inflammatory options, adequate protein
5. Practice body awareness: Before making changes based on calendar dates, check in with how you actually feel. Your unique patterns may differ from textbook descriptions.
6. Prioritize consistency over duration: During challenging phases, maintaining a shorter but consistent fasting practice often proves more beneficial than attempting longer fasts that might trigger stress responses.

Marie, a 36-year-old teacher, found this cyclical approach transformative: "I was frustrated with intermittent fasting because sometimes it felt easy and energizing, but other times I felt terrible—hungry, irritable, and foggy. Tracking my cycle revealed a clear pattern—I thrive with 18-hour fasts during my follicular phase but need to scale back to 14 hours during my luteal phase. Making this simple adjustment made fasting sustainable year-round rather than a constant struggle."

Life Stage Considerations

Beyond monthly cycles, women experience several major hormonal transitions throughout their lives that can affect their optimal fasting approach:

Perimenopause and Menopause The years surrounding menopause bring significant hormonal fluctuations that can affect metabolism, body composition, insulin sensitivity, and energy. Some considerations for this life stage:

1. Shorter fasting windows (12-14 hours) may be better tolerated initially
2. Gradual extension of fasting periods as your body adapts
3. Heightened importance of protein intake during eating windows (aim for 1.2-1.6g per kg of body weight)
4. Potential benefits from carbohydrate intake focused around exercise
5. Extra emphasis on stress management, as cortisol sensitivity often increases
6. Particular attention to sleep quality, which affects both hormonal balance and hunger

Post-Menopause After menopause, many women find their bodies respond more similarly to men's regarding fasting tolerance. This may allow for more consistent fasting patterns without the cyclical adjustments needed earlier in life. However, continued emphasis on adequate protein intake remains important for maintaining muscle mass.

Pregnancy and Breastfeeding Extended fasting is not recommended during pregnancy or while breastfeeding, as consistent energy and nutrient availability are crucial during these periods. If you become pregnant while practicing intermittent fasting, transition to regular eating patterns under your healthcare provider's guidance.

Journal Prompts: Exploring Your Body Relationship

Fasting often brings awareness to our relationship with our bodies—sometimes revealing patterns, beliefs, and emotions that have remained below the surface. These journal prompts can help you explore these insights with compassion and curiosity:

1. How would I describe my current relationship with my body? Is it primarily characterized by criticism, appreciation, frustration, or acceptance?
2. What messages did I receive growing up about women's bodies, hunger, and eating? How might these messages still influence how I approach food and fasting?
3. When I experience hunger during fasting, what emotions arise? Does hunger trigger anxiety, irritation, peace, pride, or other feelings?
4. How does fasting affect my body awareness? Am I becoming more attentive to subtle signals, or am I sometimes overriding my body's communications?
5. What have I noticed about how my energy, hunger, and mood fluctuate throughout my monthly cycle? Are there patterns I could honour more fully?
6. What would a truly nourishing approach to fasting look like—one that honours both my physical needs and my emotional wellbeing?
7. How do I distinguish between practicing healthy discipline with fasting and potentially falling into restrictive patterns that don't serve my overall health?

8. In what ways has fasting changed how I think about my body's capabilities and wisdom?

Marie found these reflections revealing: "I realized I'd been approaching fasting as another way to 'control' my body rather than work with it. Journaling helped me notice how I'd dismiss hunger during certain times in my cycle as 'weakness' rather than recognizing it as valuable information. This awareness helped me develop a more collaborative relationship with my body instead of seeing it as something to overcome or discipline."

Building a Healthier Body Relationship Through Mindful Fasting

For many women, intermittent fasting can become a pathway to a more peaceful relationship with food and body—but this outcome isn't automatic. It requires intentional practice and a mindful approach. Here are key principles for ensuring your fasting practice enhances rather than complicates your body relationship:

Honor hunger as information, not weakness: Rather than viewing hunger as an adversary to be conquered, approach it as valuable communication from your body. Sometimes the appropriate response to hunger is waiting until your eating window; other times, it's breaking your fast early because your body genuinely needs nourishment.

Distinguish between discipline and punishment: Healthy fasting comes from a place of self-care and body respect rather than punishment or extreme control. Notice the emotional tone of your practice—does it feel like caring structure or harsh restriction?

Focus on how you feel, not just how you look: Measure success through improved energy, mental clarity, emotional balance, and overall wellbeing rather than exclusively through weight or appearance changes.

Practice flexible consistency: Sustainable fasting involves holding a consistent overall pattern while allowing flexibility for your body's changing needs across cycle phases, stress levels, activity demands, and life circumstances.

Celebrate what your body can do: Use your fasting practice as an opportunity to appreciate your body's remarkable adaptability and wisdom rather than focusing on perceived flaws or limitations.

For Marie, this mindful approach created unexpected benefits: "The most surprising outcome wasn't physical but psychological. As I learned to trust my body's signals through fasting—honouring when I needed more flexibility or when I could extend my fast comfortably—I developed a level of body trust I'd never experienced before. This trust extended beyond eating patterns into how I approached exercise, rest, and even challenges in other areas of life."

Physical Activity and Exercise While Fasting

The relationship between fasting and physical activity generates perhaps more questions than any other aspect of intermittent fasting practice. Can you exercise while fasted? Should you? Does fasting affect performance? Will you lose muscle? The answers involve nuance rather than one-size-fits-all prescriptions.

Reframing Movement as Joyful Rather Than Punitive

Before addressing specific strategies, let's establish an important foundation: physical activity serves many purposes beyond calorie burning or physique changes. Movement can be a celebration of what your body can do, a source of genuine pleasure, a stress management tool, and a way to enhance overall health.

Too often, exercise becomes entangled with punishment or permission around eating—working out to "earn" food or "make up for" eating. This mentality undermines both the joy of movement and the development of a healthy relationship with food and fasting.

As you integrate exercise with your fasting practice, I encourage approaching movement with appreciation for your body's capabilities rather than as a corrective measure for your body's perceived shortcomings. This mindset shift transforms exercise from obligation to opportunity.

Fasting and Exercise: The Science

Research on fasting and exercise shows several interesting patterns:

Fat utilization increases during fasted exercise: When you exercise in a fasted state, your body relies more heavily on fat oxidation for energy compared to exercising after eating, particularly during moderate-intensity activities.

Performance effects vary by individual and exercise type: High-intensity, anaerobic activities (like heavy weight lifting or sprint intervals) may be more challenging during fasted states for some individuals due to lower glycogen availability, while moderate aerobic activities are often well-tolerated or even enhanced.

Adaptation improves capacity: Your body becomes more efficient at exercising while fasted over time. What might feel challenging initially often becomes comfortable with consistent practice as metabolic flexibility improves.

Protein synthesis and muscle preservation require attention: While fasting doesn't automatically cause muscle loss, attention to protein intake during eating windows and appropriate exercise stimulus becomes increasingly important for maintaining muscle mass.

Recovery considerations change: Nutrient timing for recovery becomes more concentrated within eating windows, requiring strategic approaches to post-exercise nutrition when combining fasting and training.

Decision Tree: Timing Workouts Relative to Fasting Periods

Determining the optimal timing for your workouts relative to your fasting schedule depends on several factors. This decision framework can help guide your approach:

Consider your primary goal:

1. Fat loss emphasis → Fasted morning exercise often beneficial
2. Performance emphasis → Exercise during or shortly before eating window often optimal
3. Muscle building emphasis → Exercise just before or during eating window typically best
4. Overall health emphasis → Personal preference and schedule convenience matter most

Consider your exercise type:
1. High-intensity resistance training → Often better tolerated during or near eating windows
2. Moderate cardio (walking, easy cycling, swimming) → Generally well-tolerated while fasted
3. High-intensity intervals → Individual response varies significantly; experiment with both timings
4. Long-duration endurance → May require nutrition strategy if extending beyond 60-90 minutes

Consider your fasting experience level:
1. New to fasting → Begin with exercise during eating windows until adaptation occurs
2. Intermediate faster → Gradually experiment with fasted workouts, starting with less intense activities
3. Experienced faster → Greater flexibility based on personal preference and response

Consider your unique response:
1. Notice energy levels, performance quality, and

recovery with different timing options
2. Pay attention to hunger response to exercise at different times
3. Track mood and enjoyment of the activity with different approaches

Try This Now: Exercise Timing Experiment

This simple experiment helps you determine your optimal workout timing relative to fasting:

1. Select a moderate exercise you can perform consistently (walking, cycling, strength training, etc.).
2. For one week, perform this exercise during your fasted state, at approximately the same intensity and duration each time. After each session, rate your:
    a. Energy level during exercise (1-10)
    b. Performance quality (1-10)
    c. Overall enjoyment (1-10)
    d. Recovery speed (1-10)
3. For the following week, perform the same exercise during your eating window, either about 1-2 hours after eating or toward the end of your eating window. Again, rate the same factors after each session.
4. Compare your ratings to identify patterns in how your body responds to different workout timing.

Many people discover clear preferences through this experiment. Marie found her results revealing: "I assumed I'd perform better exercising after eating, but my experiment showed the opposite. My morning walks and yoga in a fasted state felt energizing and clear, while the same activities after lunch left me feeling sluggish. However, for strength training, I definitely performed better when I'd eaten a couple of hours before. This simple test helped me create a schedule that works with my body instead of fighting it."

Addressing Common Concerns

Several concerns frequently arise when combining fasting and exercise. Let's address them with evidence-based perspectives and practical solutions:

Concern: Will I lose muscle while fasting? Research suggests that intermittent fasting, when implemented appropriately, doesn't cause significant muscle loss, particularly when:

1. Protein intake is adequate during eating windows (aim for at least 1.6-2.0g per kg of body weight for active individuals)
2. Resistance training provides continued stimulus for muscle maintenance
3. Overall calorie deficit (if any) is moderate rather than severe
4. Fasting periods typically remain within 16-24 hours for most practices

Practical approach: Place one of your more substantial protein-containing meals within 2-3 hours after resistance training when possible, and ensure your overall daily protein target is met within your eating window.

Concern: Will I have enough energy for effective workouts? Energy availability during fasted workouts depends on several factors:

1. Your metabolic flexibility (which improves with consistent fasting practice)
2. The type and intensity of exercise
3. Your overall nutrition quality during eating windows
4. Sleep quality and stress levels

Practical approach: If you're new to fasting, begin with lighter activities during fasted periods until adaptation occurs. For high-intensity work, consider timing these sessions during or close to your eating window initially. As adaptation improves, many find they can comfortably perform most activities while fasted.

Concern: How will fasting affect my recovery? Recovery requires adequate nutrients, hydration, and rest—all of which can be accommodated within an intermittent fasting practice:

1. Protein and carbohydrate intake can be optimized during eating windows
2. Hydration can and should continue during fasting periods
3. Sleep quality often improves with consistent fasting practices

Practical approach: If engaging in particularly demanding training, consider timing your workout shortly before your eating window opens, allowing for prompt nutritional recovery. Ensure total daily nutrition meets your activity demands, just within a compressed timeframe.

Concern: Should I take supplements while training fasted? Some supplements are compatible with fasted states while others are not:

1. Electrolytes without calories can be beneficial during fasted training
2. Branched-chain amino acids (BCAAs) technically break a fast
3. Caffeine (like black coffee) may enhance performance without breaking a fast
4. Protein supplements should be reserved for eating windows

Practical approach: For most recreational exercisers, electrolytes and water are sufficient during fasted training. Save other supplements for your eating window.

Troubleshooting Guide for Common Exercise-Fasting Challenges

Challenge: Dizziness or light-headedness during fasted workouts *If you experience these symptoms during exercise in a fasted state...*

1. Ensure proper hydration before and during exercise
2. Add electrolytes (particularly sodium) to your water
3. Consider reducing exercise intensity until better adaptation occurs
4. Check that your overall calorie intake during

eating windows is adequate
5. Try a very small amount of easily digestible carbohydrate (like a date) before exercise if symptoms persist

Challenge: Significant performance decline when fasted
If you notice substantial decrease in strength, endurance, or intensity capacity...

1. Experiment with exercise timing relative to your eating window
2. Gradually adapt with shorter fasted workouts before attempting longer sessions
3. Consider whether your total carbohydrate intake during eating windows supports your activity level
4. For high-performance goals, periodize your fasting approach with harder training days aligned with more favourable eating patterns

Challenge: Excessive hunger triggered by exercise *If workouts significantly increase hunger making fasting uncomfortable...*

1. Try scheduling intense exercise closer to the end of your fasting period
2. Experiment with different exercise intensities and durations
3. Ensure your post-workout meals contain adequate protein and fibre for satiety
4. Consider whether your overall calorie intake supports your activity level

Challenge: Poor recovery between training sessions *If you notice impaired recovery demonstrated by persistent soreness or fatigue...*

1. Review your total protein intake and distribution during eating windows
2. Assess carbohydrate intake relative to exercise demands
3. Evaluate sleep quality and stress management
4. Consider temporarily reducing either fasting strictness or training intensity until better adaptation

Challenge: Early morning workout logistics *If you struggle with timing early workouts within your fasting schedule...*

1. Consider the workout part of your fasting period rather than something requiring pre-fuelling
2. Ensure adequate nutrition the evening before
3. Hydrate well upon waking
4. Start with moderate intensities that match your current adaptation level

Marie navigated several of these challenges: "When I first tried morning runs while fasted, I felt dizzy and weak. Adding electrolytes to my water helped significantly. I also realized I wasn't eating enough carbohydrates during my eating window to support my running. Once I adjusted both these factors, my fasted morning runs actually became my favourite workouts of the week."

Creating Harmony Between Fasting and Physical Activity

The most sustainable approach integrates fasting and exercise in ways that complement rather than compete with each other. Here are principles for creating this harmony:

Align intensity with eating patterns: Higher intensity or longer duration activities often work better closer to eating windows, while moderate activities can fit comfortably within fasted periods once adapted.

Adapt progressively: Gradually introduce and extend fasted exercise as your body adapts, rather than immediately attempting your most challenging workouts while fasted.

Honor feedback: Use your body's signals—energy levels, recovery quality, hunger patterns, and performance—to guide your approach rather than following rigid prescriptions.

Periodize when appropriate: Consider adjusting both fasting and exercise patterns for different training phases if you have specific performance goals.

Prioritize consistency over intensity: Regular, moderate activity that you can maintain consistently provides greater benefits than occasional extreme sessions that require excessive recovery.

Focus on enjoyment: Choose activities you genuinely enjoy, which makes both fasting and exercise sustainable long-term components of your healthy lifestyle.

Marie found this harmonized approach transformative:

"Instead of seeing fasting and exercise as separate practices I needed to somehow force together, I began viewing them as complementary tools for overall wellbeing. Some days that means a challenging strength session followed immediately by breaking my fast with a protein-rich meal. Other days it means a peaceful fasted morning walk that actually makes the rest of my fasting period easier. The harmony comes from working with my body rather than imposing rigid rules."

Implementation Checklist: Women's Hormonal Health Considerations

For women looking to optimize fasting for hormonal health, use this checklist to create a body-supportive approach:

1. Track your cycle for at least 2-3 months, noting energy, hunger, mood, and fasting tolerance.
2. Identify your personal patterns across different cycle phases.
3. Create 2-3 different fasting approaches to rotate through based on your cycle phase.
4. Plan nutritional strategies for each phase that support hormonal balance.
5. Establish minimum fasting thresholds that feel sustainable even during challenging phases.
6. Develop clear indicators for when to modify your approach (symptoms that suggest adjustment is needed).
7. Consider supplements that support female hormonal health (with healthcare provider

guidance).
8. Prioritize sleep quality, which significantly impacts hormonal balance.
9. Implement stress management practices, as stress particularly affects female hormonal systems.
10. Schedule regular reassessment of how your fasting practice affects your cycle, energy, and wellbeing.
11. Communicate with healthcare providers about your fasting practice and any concerns.
12. Adjust your approach during major hormonal transitions like perimenopause.
13. Implementation Checklist: Exercise Optimization
14. To create an effective integration of exercise and fasting, use this checklist:
15. Experiment with workout timing relative to fasting periods to identify your optimal approach.
16. Develop hydration strategies for fasted workouts, including appropriate electrolytes.
17. Plan strategic pre-workout nutrition if exercising during eating windows.
18. Create post-workout nutrition templates that support recovery within your eating window.
19. Calculate protein needs based on your activity level and ensure adequate intake during eating windows.
20. Monitor recovery quality and adjust either fasting or exercise as needed.
21. Plan fasting flexibility around particularly demanding training sessions if necessary.

22. Implement appropriate supplements that complement your fasting and exercise goals.
23. Track performance metrics to ensure your approach supports rather than hinders progress.
24. Schedule regular movement throughout the day, not just formal exercise sessions.
25. Create contingency plans for days when energy is lower than expected.
26. Periodize both fasting and exercise if you have specific performance goals.

The integration of intermittent fasting with women's hormonal health and physical activity represents a profound opportunity to develop deeper body wisdom. By approaching these areas with both scientific understanding and personal experimentation, you create not just a fasting practice but a holistic approach to wellbeing that honours your unique physiology and needs.

As you implement the strategies in this chapter, remember that your body is remarkably adaptive and communicative. The fluctuations in your energy, hunger, and capacity aren't failures or obstacles —they're valuable information guiding you toward your most effective personal approach. By working with rather than against these natural patterns, you transform intermittent fasting from a one-size-fits-all protocol into a flexible practice that truly serves your whole health.

In our next chapter, we'll explore the inner experience of fasting—the mental clarity, emotional growth, and meaningful ways to track progress beyond the scale. These dimensions often provide the most profound and unexpected benefits of a consistent fasting practice.

CHAPTER 6: THE INNER EXPERIENCE: MENTAL CLARITY, EMOTIONAL GROWTH, AND TRACKING PROGRESS

The Unexpected Mental Revolution

When Alex began intermittent fasting, his goals were primarily physical. At 47, he wanted to lose some weight and improve his blood pressure. What he didn't anticipate was how dramatically fasting would change his mental experience.

"The first thing I noticed—even before any weight loss—was this remarkable mental clarity," Alex explained. "For years, I'd experienced this mid-morning brain fog where thinking felt like wading through mud. I'd compensated with more coffee, which helped briefly before making things worse. About ten days into practicing 16:8 fasting, I realized one morning that the fog was just... gone. My thinking was sharper than it had been in years. I could access words more easily, solve problems more creatively, and maintain focus without constantly pulling my attention back."

Alex's experience reflects one of the most commonly reported but least expected benefits of intermittent fasting—a transformation in cognitive function and emotional regulation. While many begin fasting for physical health, they often continue because of these profound mental and emotional shifts.

This cognitive enhancement isn't just subjective experience. Research increasingly supports the connection between intermittent fasting and brain function, suggesting that the same mechanisms that make fasting beneficial for physical health also promote brain health, cognitive performance, and emotional balance.

What makes these mental benefits particularly valuable is their immediacy. While physical changes like weight loss might take weeks or months to manifest, many practitioners report noticeable mental clarity within days of beginning consistent fasting. This quick positive feedback provides powerful motivation during the early adaptation phase when physical benefits remain forthcoming.

In this chapter, we'll explore the fascinating science behind fasting's effects on your brain, the emotional journey that unfolds as you change your relationship with food, practical mindfulness techniques that enhance your fasting experience, and meaningful ways to track your multidimensional progress beyond the bathroom scale.

Your Brain on Fasting: The Neuroscience of Clarity

To understand how fasting affects your brain, let's

explore the underlying mechanisms using accessible language and relatable analogies rather than technical jargon.

The Brain's Two Fuel Systems

Like your body, your brain can operate on two different fuel sources: glucose (from carbohydrates) or ketones (derived from fat). In our modern eating pattern of constant meals and snacks, most people's brains primarily run on glucose, switching to ketones only during extended sleep.

Imagine your brain as a hybrid vehicle that can run on either gasoline (glucose) or electricity (ketones). Most people only ever use the gasoline engine, unaware that they have this sophisticated electric system built in. Intermittent fasting allows your brain to regularly switch to this alternative fuel system, which many neuroscientists believe provides certain advantages for brain function.

When you fast for extended periods, typically beyond 12-14 hours, your liver begins producing ketones as blood glucose and insulin levels decrease. These ketones cross the blood-brain barrier and provide an extremely efficient energy source for your brain cells. Many people experience this metabolic switch as a noticeable clarifying effect—a transition from sluggish, foggy thinking to sharper, more focused cognition.

Neurological Spring Cleaning: BDNF and Autophagy

Beyond alternative fuel sources, fasting triggers several processes that promote brain health and function. One of the most significant is the production of Brain-

Derived Neurotrophic Factor (BDNF), often described as "fertilizer for the brain."

Think of BDNF as a rejuvenating rain shower on a garden of neural connections. It helps brain cells strengthen existing connections, form new ones, and resist deterioration. Research shows that fasting increases BDNF production, which supports cognitive function, emotional regulation, and even long-term brain health.

Simultaneously, your brain engages in heightened autophagy during fasting—the cellular self-cleaning process we discussed in earlier chapters. For your brain, this means removing damaged proteins and cellular components that could otherwise accumulate and potentially contribute to cognitive decline.

Imagine your brain cells having tiny maintenance crews that become especially active during fasting periods. These crews identify worn-out components, disassemble them, and either recycle the materials or dispose of them properly. This cleanup process helps your neurons function more efficiently and may provide protection against neurodegenerative conditions.

Inflammation Reduction and Neural Function

Chronic inflammation doesn't just affect your body—it impacts brain function too. The inflammatory markers that circulate during chronic inflammation can cross the blood-brain barrier and create what some researchers call "brain fog," reducing cognitive function and affecting mood regulation.

Intermittent fasting has been shown to reduce inflammatory markers throughout the body, including those that affect the brain. This reduction in neural inflammation often translates to clearer thinking, improved memory, and better emotional balance.

Think of inflammation as static on a radio signal—when reduced, the transmission comes through more clearly. As fasting helps lower this inflammatory static, many people experience thoughts and emotions with greater clarity and less distortion.

Stress Resistance Through Hormesis

Fasting creates a mild stress on your system—not enough to damage it, but enough to trigger adaptive responses. This beneficial stress, called hormesis, works like exercise for your brain cells, making them more resilient to other forms of stress.

Dr. Mark Mattson, a neuroscientist formerly with the National Institute on Aging and now at Johns Hopkins University, has conducted extensive research showing how this mild stress activates pathways that help neurons cope with more significant challenges. Your brain cells essentially become more stress-resistant through regular exposure to the mild stress of fasting.

Imagine your brain developing calluses, like hands that become tougher through regular work. Through intermittent fasting, your neurons develop their own form of "calluses," becoming better equipped to handle other stressors in your life.

Alex noticed this stress resilience developing: "About

a month into fasting, I realized I was responding differently to work pressure. Problems that would have sent me into a tailspin before now seemed more manageable. I had more mental space between stimulus and response—time to choose my reaction rather than just emotionally reacting."

Try This Now: The Cognitive Clarity Assessment

This simple experiment helps you objectively measure how fasting affects your mental performance:

1. Select a day when you'll be breaking a fast of at least 14-16 hours.
2. Before breaking your fast, spend 5 minutes performing these quick cognitive tests:
    a. Set a timer and write down as many animals as you can think of in 60 seconds
    b. Count backward from 100 by subtracting 7 each time (100, 93, 86...) for 30 seconds, noting how far you get
    c. Read a paragraph from a book and summarize it in your own words
    d. Rate your mental clarity on a scale of 1-10
3. After breaking your fast and waiting 60-90 minutes (allowing time for food to be digested), perform the exact same tests again.
4. Compare your performance. Many people notice significant differences in speed, accuracy, or subjective experience between their fasted and fed states.
5. Repeat this experiment 2-3 times to identify

consistent patterns in how your cognition responds to fasting and eating.

This experiment often reveals surprising cognitive patterns that you might not otherwise notice. Alex found his results eye-opening: "I was genuinely shocked by the difference. In my fasted state, I listed 31 animals compared to 24 after eating, got further in the subtraction task, and my clarity self-rating dropped from 8 to 5 after my meal. Seeing these concrete differences made me realize I wasn't imagining the cognitive benefits."

The Emotional Journey of Fasting

Perhaps even more profound than the cognitive shifts are the emotional transformations many people experience through consistent fasting. Changing when you eat inevitably changes your relationship with food, hunger, comfort, and even your sense of identity.

Facing Feelings Without Food Buffering

One of the most challenging yet ultimately rewarding aspects of fasting involves encountering emotions directly, without using food as a buffer or distraction. In our food-abundant culture, many people have unconsciously developed the habit of turning to eating whenever uncomfortable feelings arise—whether boredom, anxiety, sadness, or even happiness.

When you practice intermittent fasting, you create periods where food isn't available as an emotional coping mechanism. This unavailability creates natural opportunities to develop greater emotional awareness and alternative response strategies.

Alex found this aspect particularly transformative: "I never realized how automatically I reached for snacks when feeling stressed until fasting made that impossible during certain hours. Initially, this was uncomfortable—I'd feel the stress and have no immediate relief valve. But over time, I developed other approaches: deep breathing, brief meditation, or simply sitting with the feeling until it naturally shifted. These skills have benefited me far beyond just managing my eating habits."

The Stages of Emotional Adaptation

The emotional journey of fasting typically progresses through several stages, though individual experiences vary significantly:

Initial Resistance: Many begin with anxiety about hunger and concern about deprivation. Food thoughts may be frequent and intrusive, and emotional reactions to hunger often feel intense.

Growing Awareness: After some practice, most people begin noticing patterns in their eating triggers, distinguishing between physical and emotional hunger, and recognizing how certain emotions drive food desires.

Expanding Response Options: With continued practice, the window between emotional trigger and response gradually widens. New coping strategies develop, and the urgency of emotional eating impulses typically diminishes.

Increasing Food Freedom: Eventually, many

practitioners experience a profound shift—food remains pleasurable but holds less emotional power. Eating becomes more consciously chosen rather than reactively driven by emotions or habits.

Identity Evolution: In advanced stages, many notice shifts in how they view themselves—from "someone who needs to eat frequently" to "someone with metabolic flexibility and choice around eating." This identity shift often transfers confidence to other life areas.

This progression isn't necessarily linear, and most people cycle through these stages repeatedly, gradually spending more time in the later stages. The key insight is recognizing that emotional reactions to fasting change substantially with practice and awareness.

Journaling Prompts for Emotional Exploration

These reflective questions help illuminate your personal emotional relationship with food and fasting:

1. When I feel hungry during fasting periods, what emotions typically arise? How do these emotions change if I simply observe them with curiosity?
2. What situations or feelings most strongly trigger the desire to eat when I'm not physically hungry?
3. When I notice an urge to break my fast early without physical necessity, what's usually happening emotionally? What need am I really trying to meet?
4. How has my emotional response to hunger

changed since I began fasting? What have I learned about my relationship with discomfort?
5. What alternative strategies have I discovered for addressing emotional needs that I previously met with food?
6. How has fasting affected my sense of personal agency and self-trust? In what ways do I view my capabilities differently now?
7. What emotional patterns or habitual responses have become more visible to me through the practice of fasting?

Exploring these questions through writing often reveals insights that remain elusive through mere thinking. The act of articulating your emotional patterns creates greater awareness and opens possibilities for intentional change.

Mindfulness Practices That Enhance Fasting

The intersection of mindfulness and fasting creates a particularly powerful combination. Mindfulness—the practice of present-moment awareness without judgment—naturally complements fasting by increasing body awareness, reducing reactivity to hunger sensations, and enhancing the connection between physical and emotional experiences.

Body Scan Practice

This foundational mindfulness technique helps develop greater awareness of physical sensations, including hunger, without immediately reacting to them:

1. Find a comfortable seated or lying position in a quiet space.
2. Close your eyes and bring attention to your breath for several cycles, simply noticing the sensation of breathing.
3. Begin directing your attention systematically through your body, starting either at your head and moving downward, or at your feet and moving upward.
4. At each area, pause for 15-30 seconds, noticing any sensations present—tension, relaxation, warmth, coolness, tingling, or neutral feelings.
5. When you notice hunger sensations, observe them with particular curiosity—their location, intensity, and quality. Do they come in waves? Do they move or change?
6. If judgments or reactions arise ("This is uncomfortable, I need to eat"), simply notice these thoughts without believing or disbelieving them, then return to physical sensation.
7. Complete the scan by returning awareness to your breath, then gently open your eyes.

Practicing this scan regularly, especially during fasting periods, builds your capacity to experience hunger as interesting information rather than an emergency requiring immediate action.

Mindful Eating to Break Your Fast

How you break your fast significantly affects both physical digestion and your psychological relationship with food. This practice enhances the experience of your first meal after fasting:

1. Before eating, take three deep breaths and set an intention to eat with full awareness.
2. Look at your food with fresh eyes, as if seeing it for the first time. Notice colours, textures, steam rising, or any other visual aspects.
3. Smell your food before tasting it, noting how aroma affects your anticipation and salivation.
4. Take a small bite and pause before chewing. Notice the immediate sensations, temperature, and initial taste.
5. Chew slowly and thoroughly, observing how flavours evolve and how swallowing feels.
6. Between bites, set your utensils down and check in with your body's responses.
7. Continue eating slowly and deliberately, noticing the progression of satisfaction and fullness.

This practice transforms breaking your fast from a potentially rushed, overeager experience into a deeply satisfying ritual that often leads to naturally eating less while enjoying it more.

Try This Now: The STOP Practice for Fasting Challenges

This micro-mindfulness practice helps navigate difficult moments during fasting periods:

1. S - Stop: Whatever you're doing, pause momentarily.
2. T - Take a breath: Take one or more conscious breaths, feeling the sensations of breathing.
3. O - Observe: Notice what's happening in

your body, emotions, and thoughts without judgment. Is there physical hunger? Emotional restlessness? Habitual thoughts about food?
4. P - Proceed: Continue with your day with greater awareness, making a conscious choice about how to respond to what you observed.

This simple practice, taking just 30-60 seconds, creates a crucial space between stimulus and response. Alex found it particularly valuable: "The STOP practice became my go-to tool whenever I felt the urge to break my fast early. That small pause helped me distinguish between genuine need and habitual impulse. Sometimes I'd decide to eat—and that was fine—but often I'd realize the urge was passing, and I could comfortably continue my fast."

Tracking Progress Beyond the Scale

Perhaps nowhere is mindfulness more important than in how you measure progress on your fasting journey. The bathroom scale, while offering one type of data, provides an extremely limited perspective that can undermine your motivation and miscommunicate your actual progress.

The Limitations of Weight Measurement

Weight fluctuations often reflect changes in water, glycogen stores, and digestive contents rather than meaningful body composition changes. Particularly for women, hormonal cycles can cause weight to vary by several pounds without reflecting any actual change in body fat or muscle.

Additionally, focusing exclusively on weight can

obscure the many other valuable benefits you're gaining. When weight loss temporarily plateaus (as it naturally does), you might miss the continued improvements in other health markers, cognitive function, and emotional wellbeing.

Comprehensive Non-Scale Progress Tracker

A more meaningful approach monitors multiple dimensions of wellbeing. Rate each of these areas on a 1-10 scale weekly to track your comprehensive progress:

Physical Dimensions:
1. Energy level throughout the day
2. Sleep quality and waking refreshed
3. Hunger stability (vs. urgent hunger or crashes)
4. Digestive comfort
5. Skin clarity
6. Joint comfort and mobility
7. Recovery from exercise
8. Physical resilience (fewer minor illnesses)

Mental Dimensions:
1. Mental clarity and focus
2. Memory function
3. Cognitive stamina (mental endurance)
4. Creative thinking
5. Problem-solving ability
6. Learning capacity
7. Decision-making confidence
8. Mental flexibility

Emotional Dimensions:

1. Mood stability
2. Emotional resilience to stressors
3. General sense of wellbeing
4. Reduced anxiety
5. Positive outlook
6. Emotion regulation capacity
7. Patience and tolerance
8. Sense of calm

Behavioural Dimensions:
1. Ability to stay present
2. Response to food cues
3. Freedom from food preoccupation
4. Consistent energy for daily activities
5. Social engagement quality
6. Work performance
7. Habit consistency
8. Intuitive eating awareness

This multidimensional tracker not only provides more comprehensive progress monitoring but also highlights improvements you might otherwise overlook. Many people discover that significant positive changes are occurring even when weight remains stable.

Alex found this broader tracking transformative: "When I stopped obsessing about the scale and started tracking these other dimensions, my whole experience shifted. I noticed I was sleeping better, thinking more clearly, and feeling more emotionally balanced. My relationships improved because I wasn't getting irritable from blood sugar swings. These benefits became more motivating than any number on the scale."

Decision Point: Selecting Your Most Meaningful Progress Metrics

To identify which progress indicators matter most for your unique situation and goals, consider these questions:

1. What initially motivated you to try intermittent fasting?
    a. Weight management
    b. Specific health concerns
    c. Energy improvement
    d. Cognitive benefits
    e. Emotional balance
    f. Simplifying relationship with food
    g. Longevity interests
    h. Other personal reasons

2. Which aspects of wellbeing most directly impact your quality of life?
    a. Physical comfort and function
    b. Mental performance
    c. Emotional balance
    d. Social connection
    e. Work effectiveness
    f. Daily energy
    g. Sleep quality
    h. Other specific dimensions

3. What improvements have others noticed in you since beginning fasting?
    a. Mood changes
    b. Energy differences
    c. Presence and attention

d. Physical appearance beyond weight
e. Communication quality
f. Stress management
g. Other observed changes

4. Which benefits would keep you fasting even if your weight never changed again?
    a. Consider which non-weight benefits provide sufficient value to maintain your practice

5. What metrics can you measure objectively beyond weight?
    a. Blood pressure
    b. Blood glucose
    c. Cholesterol levels
    d. Inflammatory markers
    e. Sleep metrics
    f. Other trackable indicators

Based on your answers, select 3-5 primary progress indicators to monitor regularly. These become your personal success metrics, providing more meaningful feedback than scale weight alone.

Beyond Numbers: Non-Scale Victories That Transform Lives

The most meaningful benefits of intermittent fasting often can't be measured numerically at all. These qualitative improvements—sometimes called "non-scale victories" or NSVs—frequently create more profound life transformation than any quantifiable change.

Alex's most significant NSV emerged in his professional life: "Six months into fasting, I found myself volunteering to lead a major presentation that previously would have terrified me. The mental clarity and emotional stability I'd developed gave me confidence I'd never had before. That presentation led to a promotion that had eluded me for years—not because I'd lost weight, but because I'd gained cognitive capacity and professional presence. That kind of change doesn't show up on any scale or blood test, but it transformed my career trajectory."

Common non-scale victories reported by consistent fasting practitioners include:

Professional Advancement: Enhanced mental clarity, focus, and emotional regulation often translate to improved work performance, better presentations, more creative problem-solving, and stronger leadership presence.

Relationship Improvements: Many notice enhanced patience, presence, and emotional balance that positively affect relationships with partners, children, friends, and colleagues.

Adventure and Activity: Increased energy and physical comfort often lead to participating in activities previously avoided—hiking, dancing, traveling, or physical play with children or grandchildren.

Freedom from Food Obsession: Many long-time practitioners report a profound liberation from constant thoughts about food, meal planning, and eating timing—mental space that becomes available for more meaningful pursuits.

Clothing Comfort: Beyond smaller sizes, many notice clothes fitting differently—sitting more comfortably, not binding at the waist, or looking more flattering due to reduced inflammation and bloating.

Reclaimed Time: The reduced meal preparation, consumption, and cleanup translates to significant time savings that can be redirected toward meaningful activities.

Environmental Consciousness: Many practitioners report becoming more aware of hunger and satiety cues, naturally reducing food waste and consumption.

Identity Evolution: Perhaps most profoundly, many experience a shift in how they view themselves—from someone controlled by hunger and cravings to someone with choice, discipline, and body wisdom.

These victories, while less quantifiable than weight or blood markers, often provide the most sustainable motivation for continued practice because they directly enhance quality of life and sense of self.

Reflection Practices for Recognizing Your Progress

Regular reflection helps you recognize progress that might otherwise go unnoticed, especially changes that occur gradually. These practices help consolidate awareness of your evolving fasting journey:

Weekly Review Practice

Set aside 10-15 minutes at the end of each week to consider:

1. What physical changes or patterns have I noticed this week?
2. How has my mental performance been affected by my fasting practice?
3. What emotions have been most prominent, and how has fasting influenced my emotional landscape?
4. What has become easier about fasting compared to previous weeks?
5. What challenges have emerged or persisted, and what might help address them?
6. What am I proud of accomplishing in my fasting practice this week?
7. What adjustments might enhance my experience in the coming week?

Monthly Milestone Reflection

Monthly, conduct a more comprehensive review:

1. How has my relationship with hunger evolved over the past month?
2. What non-scale victories have I experienced that might not be immediately obvious?
3. How has my fasting practice influenced other health habits (sleep, exercise, stress management)?
4. What have I learned about my body's unique patterns and needs?
5. How has my emotional relationship with food shifted?
6. What aspects of fasting have become more intuitive or natural?
7. What support or resources might help me

continue developing my practice?
8. How might I celebrate the progress I've made while acknowledging the journey ahead?

Alex incorporated these reflections into his practice: "The weekly reviews helped me notice subtle improvements I would have missed—like how I stopped needing my afternoon coffee, or how I was handling stressful emails more calmly. The monthly reflections helped me connect these small changes to bigger life patterns. Without this deliberate reflection, I might have attributed these improvements to other factors or not noticed them at all."

Emotional Growth Checklist: Psychological Milestones in the Fasting Journey

Use this checklist to recognize significant psychological developments in your fasting practice:

1. Distinguishing physical from emotional hunger - The ability to recognize when you want to eat from true physical need versus emotional triggers.
2. Decreased hunger anxiety - Reduced fear or concern about experiencing hunger; recognizing hunger as information rather than emergency.
3. Expanded window of tolerance - Greater capacity to experience discomfort without immediate reactivity.
4. Food neutrality - Reduced moral labelling of foods as "good" or "bad"; more balanced relationship with all food types.
5. Mealtime mindfulness - Increased presence

and attention during eating; less distracted consumption.
6. Reduced food preoccupation - Decreased time spent thinking about, planning, or worrying about food and eating.
7. Body trust development - Growing confidence in your body's signals and natural wisdom around hunger and satiety.
8. Identity expansion - Shifting self-concept beyond eating habits to incorporate broader values and capabilities.
9. Emotional differentiation - Improved ability to identify specific emotions rather than using food to address general discomfort.
10. Response flexibility - Expanded repertoire of responses to stress beyond eating.
11. Comfort with uncertainty - Greater ease with changing fasting schedules, meal timing, or food availability.
12. Self-compassionate approach - The ability to adapt your fasting practice without self-criticism when circumstances require flexibility.
13. Values alignment - Fasting practice increasingly connected to deeper personal values rather than external rules or appearance concerns.
14. Integrated motivation - Shifting from extrinsic motivation (weight, appearance) to intrinsic motivation (how you feel, enhanced wellbeing).
15. Mentorship capacity - Ability to support others in their fasting journey from a place of

experience and compassion.

As you check off these milestones, celebrate them as significant achievements—often more meaningful than physical changes alone. These psychological developments frequently transfer to other life areas, creating benefits far beyond your eating patterns.

The Transformative Power of Accumulated Small Changes

The most profound transformations through fasting rarely happen overnight. Instead, they emerge from the accumulation of small, consistent changes that compound over time. Like compound interest in finance, these small improvements build upon each other, eventually creating significant life transformation.

Alex reflected on this compound effect after a year of practice: "Looking back, there was no single dramatic moment where everything changed. Instead, it was hundreds of small improvements: slightly better sleep leading to better work focus, leading to better decisions, leading to more career opportunities. Decreased inflammation leading to more comfortable movement, leading to more consistent exercise, leading to better strength and mobility. Each small change built on the previous ones, creating a life that looks dramatically different than a year ago, though the changes day-to-day were almost imperceptible."

This perspective—appreciating the power of small, consistent improvements—helps maintain motivation during plateaus or periods when progress seems slow. The cognitive clarity you experience today, the emotional balance you develop this week, the metabolic flexibility you build this month—all contribute to profound transformation over time.

As you continue your fasting journey, remember that the most valuable changes often happen beneath the surface and beyond the scale. The growing mental clarity, emotional resilience, and body wisdom you develop become foundations for greater possibility and potential in every area of life.

In the next chapter, we'll explore how fasting connects to deeper meaning through cultural traditions and spiritual practices across human history, and how your personal practice can evolve beyond physical benefits into a source of deeper insight and connection.

CHAPTER 7: FINDING MEANING: CULTURAL TRADITIONS AND DEEPENING YOUR PRACTICE

The Universal Language of Fasting

When you practice intermittent fasting, you're not just following a modern health trend. You're participating in one of humanity's oldest and most universal practices—one that spans cultures, religions, and civilizations throughout human history. There is something profoundly moving about knowing that your personal fasting experience connects you to countless others across time and geography who have engaged in this same fundamental human rhythm.

Thomas, a 55-year-old engineer who began intermittent fasting for blood sugar management, described an unexpected emotional shift after several months of practice: "I started reading about fasting traditions across different cultures and had this surprising realization—I wasn't just doing something for my health; I was participating in a practice that humans have found meaningful for thousands of years. That knowledge transformed my fasting from something purely physical into something that felt deeper and more connected. Instead of just 'not eating breakfast,' I began to see my morning fast as part of a human tradition of intentional restraint for greater clarity and purpose."

This sense of connection to something larger than ourselves often emerges naturally as a fasting practice matures. While many begin fasting purely for health benefits, the experience frequently evolves to include dimensions of meaning, purpose, and insight that extend far beyond physical wellbeing. This evolution doesn't require adopting any particular religious or spiritual framework—it simply arises from the contemplative space that fasting naturally creates in our otherwise busy lives.

In this chapter, we'll explore the rich tapestry of fasting traditions across human cultures, examine how ancient wisdom aligns with modern scientific understanding, and consider how your personal practice might evolve beyond physical health to include deeper dimensions of meaning. Whether you approach fasting from a secular, spiritual, religious, or philosophical perspective, understanding these broader contexts can enrich your experience and sustain your practice through challenges.

Fasting Across World Traditions

Virtually every major cultural and spiritual tradition includes some form of fasting. While specific approaches differ, common themes emerge across these diverse practices: intentional restraint to cultivate greater awareness, periods of abstinence to appreciate abundance, and rhythmic cycles that honour natural patterns of consumption and restraint. Let's explore some of these traditions with respect for their unique contexts and wisdom.

Islamic Fasting Traditions

Perhaps the most widely practiced fasting tradition in the modern world occurs during Ramadan, when Muslims abstain from food, drink, smoking, and other physical needs during daylight hours for an entire lunar month. This dawn-to-sunset daily fast creates a rhythm of communal fasting and feasting that brings entire communities together in shared practice.

More than mere food abstinence, Ramadan fasting aims to cultivate spiritual awareness, self-discipline, gratitude, and compassion for those less fortunate. The hunger experienced becomes a teacher, reminding practitioners of their blessings and turning attention toward spiritual rather than physical nourishment.

The iftar—the meal that breaks the fast each evening—often becomes a community event shared with family and friends. This combination of personal discipline and communal celebration creates a powerful monthly rhythm that many Muslims describe as the most meaningful period of their year.

Beyond Ramadan, many Muslims practice optional fasting on Mondays and Thursdays throughout the year, a pattern that interestingly aligns with some modern intermittent fasting approaches.

Jewish Fasting Practices

In Judaism, several fast days punctuate the calendar year, ranging from the complete 25-hour fast of Yom Kippur (the Day of Atonement) to shorter fasts commemorating historical events. These practices create a rhythm of remembrance and contemplation within the community.

Yom Kippur, the most solemn day in the Jewish calendar, involves abstaining from food and water from sunset to sunset while engaging in prayer and reflection. The physical emptiness creates space for spiritual examination, repentance, and renewal.

Other Jewish fasts include Tisha B'Av (mourning the destruction of the Temples), the Fast of Esther preceding Purim, and several minor fast days throughout the year. Each connects physical abstinence to historical remembrance and spiritual contemplation.

Christian Fasting Traditions

Christian traditions include various fasting practices, though these have diminished in many modern denominations. Historically, seasons like Lent (the 40 days before Easter) involved significant dietary restrictions, often abstaining from meat, dairy, and other foods while embracing simpler meals.

Orthodox Christian traditions maintain more rigorous fasting practices, with scheduled fast days comprising over half the calendar year. These include abstention from animal products on Wednesdays and Fridays, longer fasts during Lent and Advent, and special fasts before major feast days.

In many Christian traditions, fasting is coupled with prayer and almsgiving (charity)—a three-part practice aimed at reorienting the practitioner away from self-indulgence and toward God and neighbour. The hunger felt during fasting serves as a physical reminder to turn toward spiritual nourishment and compassionate action.

Hindu Fasting Customs

Hindu traditions include numerous fasting practices, varying by region, deity, personal vow, and occasion. These range from complete abstention from food and water to selective fasting from particular foods.

Many Hindus observe regular weekly fasts, such as Monday fasts dedicated to Lord Shiva or Friday fasts honouring the goddess Lakshmi. Monthly fasts often align with lunar cycles, while annual fasts accompany major festivals.

Unlike some traditions where the fast is identical for all practitioners, Hindu fasting often involves personalized practices based on individual devotion and vows (vratas). The personalized nature of these fasts reflects the importance of individual spiritual relationship within broader community practices.

Buddhist Approaches to Moderation

Buddhism emphasizes the "Middle Way" between indulgence and extreme asceticism. While the Buddha rejected the severe fasting he practiced before his enlightenment, many Buddhist traditions incorporate moderate eating restrictions.

One common practice, particularly in monastic settings, involves eating only in the morning and early afternoon, abstaining from food from noon until the next day. This naturally creates a daily intermittent fasting pattern similar to contemporary time-restricted eating.

The purpose extends beyond physical health to cultivating mindfulness, reducing attachment to sensual pleasures, and creating mental clarity for meditation practice. The physical sensation of hunger becomes an opportunity to observe craving and attachment without immediately responding—a practical application of core Buddhist principles.

Indigenous Fasting Practices

Many indigenous cultures worldwide incorporate fasting into significant life transitions and spiritual practices. Vision quests among various Native American traditions often involve fasting in nature, creating space for insights, guidance, and connection with the spiritual world.

These practices typically view hunger not as deprivation but as an opening—a thinning of the veil between ordinary and non-ordinary reality that facilitates deeper connection with oneself, the natural world, and spiritual dimensions of existence.

In many indigenous traditions, fasting occurs within a community context, with elders guiding the process and the community supporting the individual through their journey and honouring their insights upon return.

Philosophical Traditions and Secular Fasting

Beyond explicitly religious contexts, many philosophical traditions have advocated fasting for mental clarity, self-discipline, and ethical development. Stoic philosophers like Seneca recommended periodic voluntary simplicity, including food restriction, to cultivate resilience and appreciation.

Socrates and Plato discussed the benefits of occasional hunger for maintaining clear thinking and philosophical insight. Enlightenment philosophers later revisited these classical ideas, exploring how physical restraint might contribute to clearer reasoning and ethical behaviour.

In the modern secular context, fasting has been embraced by various philosophical movements focused on simplicity, environmental sustainability, and conscious consumption. These approaches emphasize how temporary abstention from food can heighten awareness of privilege, consumption patterns, and connection to natural cycles.

Ancient Wisdom Meets Modern Science

One of the most fascinating aspects of studying traditional fasting practices is recognizing how many empirically discovered patterns align with contemporary scientific findings. Without modern technology or metabolic research, cultures worldwide developed fasting protocols that science now confirms provide significant health benefits.

Cyclic Eating Patterns

Nearly all traditional fasting practices involve cyclical rather than continuous fasting—periods of restriction followed by periods of normal or even celebratory eating. Modern research on intermittent fasting suggests this cycling between metabolic states may deliver greater benefits than continuous caloric restriction or continuous feeding.

Dr. Satchin Panda's research on circadian rhythms and time-restricted eating scientifically validates what many religious traditions empirically discovered—that confining eating to certain daylight hours while fasting during evening and night creates beneficial metabolic effects.

Metabolic Flexibility

Traditional cultures recognized that periods without food seemed to increase resilience and adaptability. We now understand this scientifically as improved metabolic flexibility—the body's ability to switch efficiently between using carbohydrates and fats for fuel.

Cognitive Clarity

Across traditions, fasting has been associated with mental clarity, insight, and spiritual receptivity. Modern neuroscience confirms that fasting influences brain function through several mechanisms, including ketone production, BDNF increase, and reduced inflammation—all contributing to enhanced cognitive function.

Community and Accountability

Traditional fasting practices rarely occurred in isolation—they were typically community endeavours with shared timing, mutual support, and collective breaking of fasts. Contemporary research confirms that social support significantly improves adherence to health practices, including intermittent fasting.

Thomas found this convergence between ancient wisdom and modern science particularly meaningful: "Learning that science was validating practices that humans had followed for thousands of years deepened my respect for traditional wisdom. It wasn't just that ancient cultures had stumbled upon something beneficial—they had developed sophisticated fasting approaches that modern science is only now beginning to understand fully."

Comparative Chart: Traditional Wisdom and Scientific Findings

Traditional Fasting Insight	Modern Scientific Understanding
Fasting periods create mental clarity	Ketones provide efficient brain fuel; BDNF increases during fasting; reduced neuroinflammation
Cyclic fasting and feasting more sustainable than constant deprivation	Metabolic switching between fed and fasted states provides greater benefits than continuous restriction
Fasting increases spiritual receptivity and awareness	Altered brain states during extended fasting include increased focus, reduced

	external stimulation response
Fasting builds resilience to hardship	Hormetic stress response strengthens cellular resistance to various stressors
Communal fasting provides better adherence than individual efforts	Social support significantly improves health behaviour adherence
Seasonal fasting aligns with natural cycles	Circadian rhythm research shows timing of food intake significantly impacts metabolic health
Fasting creates appreciation for food when breaking fast	Heightened taste perception and satisfaction occur after fasting periods

This convergence doesn't suggest that traditional practices were developed with scientific understanding, but rather that empirical wisdom accumulated through centuries of human experience often anticipated what science would later confirm. Both traditional wisdom and modern science offer valuable perspectives on the multidimensional benefits of fasting.

Beyond Physical Benefits: The Evolving Fasting Journey

For many practitioners, a fascinating evolution occurs as their fasting practice matures. What begins as a primarily physical health intervention gradually expands to include psychological, emotional, and even spiritual dimensions. This natural progression often unfolds through several stages:

The Typical Evolution of Fasting Practice

Stage 1: Mechanistic Focus Initially, most practitioners approach fasting with attention to schedules, rules, and physiological mechanics. The focus centers largely on "doing it right" and achieving specific physical outcomes. This stage is characterized by tracking hours, carefully monitoring allowed beverages, and attention to the technical aspects of fasting.

Stage 2: Personal Pattern Recognition As practice continues, awareness naturally expands to include your unique patterns and responses. You begin noticing not just what happens during fasting but how these experiences connect to your specific body, psychology, and life circumstances. The rigid rules often soften as personal wisdom grows.

Stage 3: Integration With Life Rhythm Eventually, fasting becomes less of a separate health practice and more integrated with your overall life rhythm. Rather than requiring constant attention and effort, it becomes a natural pattern that flows with your work, relationships, and activities. Decisions about fasting timing become more intuitive and contextual.

Stage 4: Contemplative Dimension For many long-term practitioners, fasting eventually opens contemplative dimensions—creating space for deeper questions about purpose, values, relationship with consumption, and connection to larger natural and cultural patterns. The practice becomes a vehicle for insight beyond physical health.

Stage 5: Meaningful Ritual At its most evolved, fasting can become meaningful ritual—a practice that connects you to deeper values, broader human experience, and the natural rhythms of feast and fast that have shaped human evolution. This doesn't require religious belief, simply recognition of how intentional practices carry meaning beyond their mechanical function.

Thomas described his journey through these stages: "I started with spreadsheets tracking my fasting hours and allowed beverages—completely focused on rules and outcomes. Now, three years later, my practice flows naturally with my life's rhythm. The quiet morning hours while fasting have become my time for reflection, clarity, and setting intentions for the day. The physical benefits remain important, but they're just one dimension of what fasting has become for me—a practice that brings me into greater awareness of my life, choices, and connections."

Try This Now: Contemplative Fasting Reflection

This simple reflective practice helps explore the contemplative dimension of your fasting experience:

1. Choose a day when you'll be fasting for at least 16 hours.
2. Approximately 12-14 hours into your fast, find 15 quiet minutes in a comfortable location with minimal distractions.
3. Begin with three deep breaths, allowing your attention to settle into your body.
4. Notice the sensations of fasting in your

body without judgment—perhaps emptiness, lightness, occasional hunger signals, or clear-headedness.
5. Consider these reflection questions, spending about 2-3 minutes with each:
    a. What space—physical, mental, or emotional—has opened in my life through the practice of fasting?
    b. How does temporarily abstaining from food affect my appreciation when I do eat?
    c. What patterns of consumption, beyond just food, have I become more aware of through fasting?
    d. How does this practice connect me to others who fast, either now or throughout human history?
6. Conclude by setting an intention for how you might bring awareness from this fasting period into your next meal and the remainder of your day.

This practice helps develop the contemplative muscle that many find becomes a natural and valuable dimension of mature fasting practice. The insights that emerge often extend far beyond eating patterns to influence other life choices and perspectives.

Finding Your Personal Fasting Philosophy

As your practice deepens, you may find yourself naturally developing a personal fasting philosophy—a framework of meaning that transcends mechanical health benefits. This philosophy need not be borrowed wholesale from any tradition but can authentically emerge from your own experience, values, and worldview.

Elements to Consider in Your Personal Philosophy

Relationship with Consumption: Many practitioners find fasting naturally raises questions about their overall relationship with consumption—not just food but all resources. How might periodic abstention from eating inform more conscious consumption in other areas?

Appreciation and Gratitude: Regular fasting often heightens appreciation for food when eating resumes. This gratitude may extend beyond food to other aspects of life that fasting helps you not take for granted.

Relationship with Discomfort: Fasting creates manageable, time-limited discomfort that many find builds capacity for navigating other life challenges with greater equanimity.

Simplicity and Attention: The simplification that fasting brings—fewer decisions about food, fewer eating occasions—often creates space for heightened attention to what remains.

Connection to Natural Rhythms: Alternating between fasting and eating creates a rhythm that many find reconnects them to natural cycles of effort and rest, consumption and abstention.

Community and Shared Practice: Even when practicing independently, awareness of others engaging in similar fasting practices throughout time and across cultures can create a sense of meaningful connection.

Reflection Questions That Help Define Your Philosophy

These questions help articulate your emerging personal philosophy around fasting:

1. Beyond physical health, what value do I find in temporarily abstaining from food?
2. What insights about myself have emerged through my fasting practice?
3. How has fasting affected my relationship with food during eating periods?
4. What parallels do I see between fasting discipline and other areas of my life?
5. How might my fasting practice connect to my broader values and priorities?
6. What meaning do I find in participating in a practice shared across human cultures and history?
7. How does fasting influence my sense of what I genuinely need versus what I habitually want?

Thomas discovered his personal philosophy through such reflection: "I realized my fasting practice had become a regular reminder of the difference between genuine needs and habitual wants—not just with food but in all areas of life. This awareness has influenced my purchasing decisions, how I spend my time, even the career direction I'm now pursuing. What began as a health practice has become a regular invitation to question what truly matters and what's just momentary craving."

Cultural Appreciation Without Appropriation

As you develop your personal fasting philosophy, you may feel drawn to elements from various cultural or religious traditions. Approaching these with respect and proper context is important:

Learn and Acknowledge Sources: If you incorporate elements from specific traditions, learn about their context and acknowledge their origins rather than presenting them as personal discoveries.

Respect Boundaries: Some religious or cultural fasting practices are reserved for members of those communities. Appreciate them from the outside rather than adopting them without invitation or proper preparation.

Find Universal Elements: Many aspects of fasting transcend specific cultural contexts—the experience of hunger, clarity through simplicity, appreciation through temporary abstention. These universal human experiences can form the core of your personal practice.

Seek Authentic Connection: If a particular tradition deeply resonates with you, consider learning from its authentic sources and practitioners rather than adapting isolated elements.

Develop Your Own Authentic Practice: The most meaningful approach combines respect for traditional wisdom with honesty about your own context and experience, creating a practice that authentically reflects your journey.

Signs of Readiness for Advanced Fasting Approaches

As your fasting practice matures, you may feel drawn to explore more extended fasting periods or different fasting approaches. This evolution should emerge naturally from experience rather than being forced by external standards. Here are signs that might indicate readiness for more advanced exploration:

Self-Assessment Tool: Readiness for Advanced Fasting

Rate your experience with each indicator from 1 (rarely) to 5 (consistently):

Physiological Readiness ▫ Your current fasting practice feels physically comfortable and sustainable ▫ You've developed strong metabolic flexibility with stable energy ▫ Your hunger signals have become more predictable and manageable ▫ You recover well from your current fasting periods ▫ You've resolved initial adaptation challenges like headaches or excessive hunger

Psychological Readiness ▫ You approach fasting with curiosity rather than rigid rules ▫ You can distinguish between habitual eating urges and genuine body needs ▫ You have effective strategies for managing fasting discomfort ▫ You maintain emotional balance during extended fasting periods ▫ You can adjust your fasting approach without self-judgment when circumstances require it

Lifestyle Integration ▫ Your fasting practice works harmoniously with your social and family life ▫ You've successfully navigated various life circumstances while maintaining your practice ▫ You have support systems in place for more advanced exploration ▫ Your current fasting schedule integrates well with your work and responsibilities ☐ You've established consistent sleep, hydration, and other supporting health practices

Deeper Purpose ☐ You have clear intention for exploring more advanced approaches beyond novelty ☐ You approach extended fasting with respect for your body's signals ☐ You're interested in the contemplative dimensions of longer fasts ☐ You have specific goals or questions that extended fasting might address ☐ You've researched and understand the physical processes of longer fasts

If you score predominantly 4-5 in most categories, you likely have the foundation for exploring more advanced fasting approaches. Scores of 1-3 in any category suggest areas to develop further before significantly extending your fasting periods.

Advanced Approaches to Consider

When the foundation is solid, you might explore:

24-Hour Fasts: A full day of fasting, perhaps once weekly, which allows deeper metabolic effects while remaining manageable for many experienced practitioners.

Alternate-Day Modified Fasting: Alternating between normal eating days and modified fasting days (with minimal calorie intake), which research suggests offers significant metabolic and autophagy benefits.

Extended Fasting (2-5 days): Longer fasting periods that promote more profound autophagy and cellular cleanup. These require proper preparation, careful refeeding, and should be approached gradually.

Fasting Mimicking Diet: Developed by Dr. Valter Longo, this approach provides minimal specific nutrients that maintain many fasting benefits while reducing some challenges of water-only extended fasting.

Seasonal Fasting Intensity: Some practitioners align more intensive fasting periods with seasonal transitions, similar to many traditional practices that included seasonal fasting observations.

Thomas approached advanced fasting methodically: "After about 18 months of consistent 16:8 and 18:6 fasting, I felt ready to explore a monthly 24-hour fast. I prepared carefully, scheduled it when I had minimal obligations, and approached it as a learning experience rather than an achievement to complete. That monthly practice has now become a valuable rhythm—a regular reset that provides both physical benefits and contemplative space that the daily practice doesn't quite create."

Meaningful Practice Checklist: Integrating Deeper Dimensions

Use this checklist to develop the meaningful dimensions of your fasting practice:

1. Create intentional transitions between fasting and eating periods, perhaps through a moment of gratitude or reflection.
2. Develop a personal ritual for breaking fasts that honours the experience and creates mindful transition.

3. Explore the history and traditions of fasting in cultures or spiritual traditions that interest you.
4. Connect with community, either in-person or online, who approach fasting with similar values.
5. Journal regularly about insights, questions, or awareness that emerges during fasting periods.
6. Notice connections between your fasting discipline and other life areas where similar principles might apply.
7. Align fasting patterns with natural rhythms like seasons, lunar cycles, or personal biorhythms that feel meaningful.
8. Create designated contemplative time during longer fasts for reflection, meditation, or simply being present with the experience.
9. Develop gratitude practices specifically connected to your fasting and eating cycle.
10. Consider fasting's relationship to your broader values like environmental sustainability, spiritual practice, or conscious consumption.
11. Share your experience thoughtfully with others who might benefit, respecting different approaches and perspectives.
12. Periodically review and refine your personal fasting philosophy as your experience deepens.

Finding Your Meaningful Path

As we conclude this exploration of fasting's deeper dimensions, remember that meaning emerges primarily through personal experience rather than external prescription. While traditional and cultural practices offer valuable wisdom, your most sustainable and meaningful fasting practice will ultimately be the one that authentically aligns with your unique values, body, and life context.

Thomas reflected on this personalized journey: "What's been most surprising is how my fasting practice has evolved into something I couldn't have predicted when I started. It began as a health intervention but has become a cornerstone practice that influences how I approach consumption, attention, discipline, and appreciation in all areas of life. The physical benefits remain important, but the perspective shifts have been even more valuable."

Whether you're drawn to fasting for purely health reasons, find meaning in connecting to ancient human traditions, integrate fasting with specific spiritual practices, or simply appreciate the clarity and intention it brings to your relationship with consumption—the path you create will be uniquely yours.

The beauty of intermittent fasting lies in this versatility: the same physiological practice can carry different meanings for different practitioners while delivering similar health benefits. Some find profound spiritual significance in fasting; others appreciate its philosophical dimensions; still others value the practical benefits while finding meaning in the self-discipline it develops.

All of these approaches are valid. The invitation of this chapter isn't to adopt any specific meaningful framework but to remain open to the dimensions beyond physical health that may naturally emerge as your practice matures. By bringing awareness to these deeper aspects, you transform what might otherwise be simply another health habit into a practice that nourishes not just your body but your whole self.

In our next chapter, we'll address the crucial aspects of safety and support—ensuring your fasting practice remains physically appropriate while building the connections that enhance sustainability and enjoyment.

CHAPTER 8: STAYING SAFE AND FINDING SUPPORT

Safety as the Foundation of Sustainable Practice

Before diving into specific safety considerations, I want to emphasize a fundamental principle that guides everything in this chapter: your fasting practice should enhance your wellbeing, not compromise it. This might seem obvious, but in a health culture that sometimes glorifies extreme approaches or suggests that discomfort equals effectiveness, this principle bears repeating.

Intermittent fasting is not about testing how long you can endure hunger or pushing your body to its limits. It's about creating a sustainable rhythm that works with your body's natural processes to improve health and quality of life. Safety isn't an optional add-on to your practice—it's the foundation upon which everything else rests.

Sophia, a 42-year-old marketing executive and mother of two, learned this lesson through experience. "When I first started intermittent fasting, I pushed too hard too fast," she explained. "I jumped straight into 20:4 fasting because I thought more extreme meant better results. I ignored signals like dizziness and trouble concentrating because I thought that was just part of the process.

It took a conversation with my doctor to help me understand that those symptoms weren't badges of honour—they were my body telling me to adjust my approach."

Like Sophia, many beginners mistake warning signs for adjustment symptoms or view safety precautions as obstacles to overcome rather than wisdom to respect. This chapter aims to help you develop both the knowledge and the self-awareness to practice fasting in ways that truly serve your health rather than potentially compromising it.

Important Medical Disclaimer

The information in this book, including this chapter, is educational in nature and not intended as medical advice. Intermittent fasting may not be appropriate for everyone, and the guidance provided here cannot replace personalized recommendations from healthcare providers familiar with your specific medical history, current health status, and individual needs.

Before beginning intermittent fasting, especially if you have existing health conditions or take medications, consult with qualified healthcare professionals such as your primary care physician, specialist providers for any conditions you have, or a registered dietitian with knowledge of intermittent fasting.

This consultation is particularly important if you:

1. Have diabetes or blood sugar regulation issues
2. Take prescription medications, especially

those requiring food
3. Have a history of eating disorders
4. Are pregnant or breastfeeding
5. Are under 18 or over 65
6. Have chronic medical conditions like heart disease, kidney disease, or liver disease
7. Have hormonal imbalances or conditions
8. Are underweight or have nutritional deficiencies

While intermittent fasting offers benefits for many people, individual responses vary significantly. Your health and safety should always take precedence over adherence to any particular fasting protocol or schedule.

Understanding Contraindications and Caution Areas

Some health conditions and life situations make fasting either inappropriate or requiring significant modification and medical supervision. Understanding these contraindications helps you make informed decisions about whether and how to incorporate fasting into your life.

When Fasting Is Not Recommended

Pregnancy and Breastfeeding: These states require consistent energy and nutrient intake to support the developing baby or milk production. Extended fasting periods are not recommended during these times.

Active Eating Disorders or History of Eating Disorders: The structured eating limitations of intermittent fasting can potentially trigger or exacerbate disordered eating patterns and unhealthy relationships with food.

Type 1 Diabetes: Fasting with Type 1 diabetes requires extremely careful medical management due to risks of dangerous blood sugar fluctuations. It should only be attempted under close medical supervision with providers experienced in both diabetes management and fasting.

Underweight Status or Malnutrition: Those who are underweight (BMI below 18.5) or have nutritional deficiencies should focus on consistent nutrient intake rather than restricting eating windows.

Children and Adolescents: Young, growing bodies generally need regular nutrition throughout the day. Fasting is typically not recommended for those under 18 years of age.

Advanced Age with Frailty: Elderly individuals, particularly those with frailty or muscle wasting, often benefit more from regular protein intake throughout the day rather than extended fasting periods.

Conditions Requiring Medical Supervision

Type 2 Diabetes: While many with Type 2 diabetes practice fasting successfully, it requires careful monitoring and often medication adjustments, particularly for those taking insulin or sulfonylureas.

Cardiovascular Disease: Those with existing heart conditions should consult with their cardiologist before beginning fasting, especially if taking medications that affect heart rate or blood pressure.

Kidney Disease: Fasting can affect kidney function and electrolyte balance, requiring careful monitoring for those with existing kidney issues.

Liver Disease: The liver plays a crucial role during fasting metabolism; those with liver conditions need specialized guidance.

Thyroid Disorders: Fasting can affect thyroid function in some individuals, requiring monitoring and potentially adjustment of thyroid medications.

Gout: Fasting can temporarily increase uric acid levels, potentially triggering gout flares in susceptible individuals.

Taking Prescription Medications: Many medications are designed to be taken with food or have timing recommendations related to meals. Fasting may require medication schedule adjustments that should only be made in consultation with healthcare providers.

Safety Reference Chart: Special Considerations for Specific Populations

For your quick reference, here's a chart outlining how different conditions might affect fasting approaches:

Condition/Situation	Fasting Approach	Key Considerations
Healthy adults	Standard approaches generally safe	Start gradually, adjust based on response
Type 2 Diabetes	Medical supervision required	Medication timing may need adjustment; blood glucose monitoring essential
Hypertension	Medical consultation advised	May require blood pressure medication adjustments

History of hypoglycemia	Cautious approach with shorter fasts initially	Symptoms monitoring crucial; keep fast-breaking food available
Taking medications	Medical consultation required	Many medications require specific food timing
History of gallstones	Medical consultation advised	Rapid weight loss can increase stone formation
Gastroesophageal reflux	Individual response varies	Some find improvement with fasting; others need food to buffer stomach acid
Migraine sufferers	Individualized approach	Some find fasting triggers migraines; others experience reduction
Menstruating women	Cyclical approach recommended	Consider shorter fasts during luteal phase
Athletes	Timing around training essential	Consider performance and recovery needs
Older adults (65+)	Gentler approaches typically better	Special attention to protein intake and muscle preservation
Shift workers	Adapt to sleep schedule, not clock time	Consistency within rotation periods rather than fixed times

The Role of Healthcare Providers

Finding knowledgeable healthcare support for your fasting practice can significantly enhance both safety and effectiveness. Unfortunately, not all medical professionals are equally familiar with current research on intermittent fasting, which can make finding appropriate guidance challenging.

Finding Knowledgeable Medical Support

When seeking healthcare providers who can effectively support your fasting practice, consider these approaches:

Ask about fasting experience: Directly inquire whether providers have experience working with patients practicing intermittent fasting and their general approach to it.

Seek functional or integrative practitioners: Doctors and healthcare providers who practice functional or integrative medicine often have more training in nutritional approaches like intermittent fasting.

Connect with fasting-aware specialists: If you have specific conditions requiring specialist care, look for specialists who recognize fasting as a legitimate health tool rather than dismissing it outright.

Consider registered dietitians with fasting knowledge: Many registered dietitians now specialize in intermittent fasting and can provide nutritional guidance that complements your medical care.

Ask for recommendations: Online and in-person fasting communities often share information about healthcare providers who are knowledgeable and supportive about fasting approaches.

Sophia found this approach valuable: "I specifically asked potential new primary care doctors about their familiarity with intermittent fasting during initial consultations. The difference in responses was illuminating—some dismissed it immediately, while others engaged thoughtfully with how it might work with my specific health situation. I chose a doctor who was both knowledgeable and open-minded, which made a huge difference in receiving appropriate guidance."

Healthcare Partnership Guide: Having Productive Conversations

Regardless of your provider's initial familiarity with fasting, you can foster productive conversations by preparing effectively:

1. Bring specific information: Rather than vague statements about wanting to try fasting, share the specific approach you're considering, including fasting durations and frequency.
2. Connect to medical goals: Frame fasting in relation to specific health markers you and your provider are working to improve, such as insulin sensitivity or inflammation.
3. Request monitoring: Suggest appropriate lab work or check-ins to monitor your response to fasting, demonstrating your commitment to safety.
4. Ask specific questions: Prepare questions about how fasting might interact with your particular health conditions or medications rather than seeking general approval.
5. Share reliable resources: If your provider seems unfamiliar with current fasting research, respectfully offer to share evidence-based resources they might review.
6. Propose a trial period: Suggest a defined trial period with appropriate monitoring as a way to assess your individual response rather than making an indefinite commitment.

Sample Conversation Script with Healthcare Providers

Here's how you might approach a conversation with your healthcare provider:

"I've been researching intermittent fasting and am interested in trying a 16:8 approach, where I'd eat during an 8-hour window each day and fast for the remaining 16 hours. From my understanding, this might help improve my insulin sensitivity and reduce inflammation, which could support our goal of managing my [specific health concern].

I'd like to try this approach for 6-8 weeks while monitoring how it affects my [relevant health markers]. What specific concerns would you have about me trying this given my health history? Are there particular symptoms I should watch for, or modifications you'd recommend to make this safer for my situation?

Would you be comfortable with me checking in after a month to review how it's affecting me and any blood work or other monitoring you think would be appropriate?"

Decision Point: When to Seek Medical Guidance About Fasting

Use this framework to determine when medical consultation is appropriate regarding your fasting practice:

1. Are you in a clearly contraindicated category?
    a. Pregnancy or breastfeeding
    b. Active eating disorder or recent history of one

c. Under age 18 or elderly with frailty
   d. Significantly underweight → If yes to any, consult healthcare provider before considering fasting

2. Do you have medical conditions requiring management?
   a. Diabetes (Type 1 or 2)
   b. Heart disease or high blood pressure
   c. Kidney or liver disease
   d. Hormonal disorders
   e. History of eating disorders → If yes to any, seek medical guidance before beginning fasting

3. Do you take prescription medications?
   a. Medications for diabetes or blood sugar
   b. Blood pressure medications
   c. Medications that specify taking with food
   d. Multiple daily medications → If yes, consult with your prescribing provider about timing and adjustments

4. Have you experienced concerning symptoms while fasting?
   a. Dizziness or fainting
   b. Unusual heart rhythms or palpitations
   c. Severe headaches
   d. Significant weakness or fatigue
   e. Persistent digestive distress → If yes, consult healthcare provider before

continuing fasting

5. Are you planning to significantly intensify your fasting practice?
   a. Moving from daily time-restricted eating to extended fasts (24+ hours)
   b. Increasing fasting frequency substantially
   c. Combining fasting with other significant dietary changes → If yes, consider medical consultation, especially with underlying health concerns

Remember that consulting healthcare providers isn't a sign of weakness or unnecessary caution—it's a mark of wisdom and self-care. The most successful fasting practitioners are those who integrate appropriate medical guidance into their approach.

The Emotional Importance of Social Support

While medical safety forms the foundation of sustainable fasting, social and emotional support creates the structure that helps your practice endure through challenges. Research consistently shows that people making lifestyle changes with adequate social support are significantly more likely to maintain those changes long-term compared to those attempting changes in isolation.

Building Your Support System

Effective support for your fasting practice can come from various sources, each offering different benefits:

Close Personal Relationships: Partners, family members, and close friends who understand and encourage your fasting practice can provide daily reinforcement and practical assistance.

Peers on Similar Journeys: Connecting with others practicing intermittent fasting creates opportunities for sharing specific strategies, normalizing experiences, and mutual encouragement through challenges.

Professional Support: Healthcare providers, nutritionists, or coaches with fasting expertise can offer structured guidance, accountability, and troubleshooting when obstacles arise.

Online Communities: Virtual groups focused on intermittent fasting provide accessible support, diverse perspectives, and often around-the-clock encouragement regardless of your location.

Workplace Connections: Colleagues who understand your eating schedule can help create accommodating environments and reduce workplace food pressure.

The most robust support systems typically include multiple types of support rather than relying exclusively on one source. This diversification ensures that if one support source becomes temporarily unavailable, others remain to sustain your practice.

Visual Support System Map Tool

To identify and strengthen your support network, create a visual map using this structure:

    1. Draw a circle in the centre with your name.

2. Create four quadrants around your circle labelled: Family/Household, Friends/Social, Professional/Workplace, and Community/Online.
3. In each quadrant, write names of specific people or groups who could potentially support your fasting practice.
4. Next to each name, note:
    a. Current support level (Supportive, Neutral, Challenging)
    b. Type of support they could best provide (Practical, Emotional, Informational)
    c. Action needed to strengthen this support connection
5. Identify gaps in your support system—quadrants with few names or types of support currently missing.
6. Develop a plan to strengthen at least one support connection in each quadrant.

This visual mapping helps you recognize existing resources while strategically developing areas where support might be lacking.

Finding and Evaluating Communities

Community support specifically focused on intermittent fasting can provide specialized encouragement, troubleshooting, and camaraderie that general relationships might not offer.

Curated List of Reputable Support Resources

While specific online communities and resources

continually evolve, here are categories of support to explore:

Moderated Online Forums: Look for forums with active moderators who enforce respectful communication and evidence-based information. These spaces typically provide more reliable information than unmoderated groups.

Professional-Led Communities: Some healthcare providers, registered dietitians, and wellness coaches host fasting communities with professional oversight, combining social support with expert guidance.

App-Based Communities: Several fasting-focused apps include community features where you can connect with others following similar protocols while tracking your own practice.

Local Meetup Groups: In some areas, in-person groups focused on intermittent fasting or general metabolic health meet regularly to share experiences and support.

Evidence-Based Educational Communities: Some online platforms focus primarily on sharing current research and evidence-based approaches rather than personal anecdotes.

Digital Community Evaluation Tool

Not all fasting communities provide healthy, evidence-based support. Use these criteria to evaluate potential communities before deeply engaging:

Information Quality:

    1. Does the community share evidence-based

information with references?
2. Are scientific claims verified rather than based on personal anecdotes alone?
3. Is there nuance in discussions rather than absolute claims?
4. Are diverse perspectives welcomed within evidence-based parameters?

Moderation and Safety:
1. Are there clear community guidelines promoting respectful communication?
2. Do moderators actively ensure discussions remain supportive and accurate?
3. Is dangerous advice promptly corrected or removed?
4. Are medical disclaimers appropriately emphasized?

Support Atmosphere:
1. Is the tone generally positive and encouraging rather than judgmental?
2. Do members receive support during both successes and struggles?
3. Is there respect for individual differences in approaches?
4. Do responses to questions demonstrate patience and helpfulness?

Diversity and Inclusivity:
1. Are diverse experiences and backgrounds welcomed and represented?
2. Is there recognition that approaches may need to vary for different people?
3. Are there discussions relevant to various

life circumstances (different ages, health conditions, etc.)?
4. Is weight stigma or body shaming discouraged?

Red Flags to Watch For:
1. Promotion of extreme fasting approaches without safety considerations
2. One-size-fits-all recommendations regardless of individual circumstances
3. Dismissal of medical guidance or encouragement to ignore doctor recommendations
4. Selling products as necessary for successful fasting
5. Cult-like devotion to specific protocols or group leaders
6. Shaming of members who modify their approach or express concerns

Sophia found this evaluation process crucial: "I initially joined a fasting group that seemed supportive but gradually noticed concerning patterns—members were encouraged to push through dizziness and fatigue, and anyone mentioning consulting their doctor was dismissed as not being committed enough. I left and found a community with medical professionals among the membership who provided evidence-based guidance alongside peer support. The difference in my fasting experience was dramatic."

Navigating Conversations with Others

Even with supportive communities in place, you'll

inevitably face conversations about your fasting practice with people who may be sceptical, concerned, or simply curious. These interactions can range from mildly uncomfortable to genuinely challenging, especially with people who play significant roles in your life.

Approaching Different Types of Conversations

Casual Inquiries: For general questions from acquaintances or colleagues, brief, matter-of-fact responses usually suffice. "I've found eating this way helps my energy and focus" typically satisfies curiosity without inviting unwanted opinions.

Concerned Questions: When loved ones express worry, acknowledge their care while providing reassurance. "I appreciate your concern. I've researched this carefully and consulted my doctor to make sure it's appropriate for my health situation."

Sceptical Challenges: For those who question the validity of fasting, decide whether the relationship merits detailed explanation. Sometimes a simple "This approach is working well for me, though I understand it's not for everyone" maintains boundaries while respecting different viewpoints.

Persistent Criticism: With repeated negative comments, clearer boundaries become necessary. "I understand you have different opinions about this, but I've made an informed decision and would prefer not to discuss my eating patterns further."

Genuinely Interested Inquiries: When someone shows authentic interest in understanding your practice, sharing your personal experience and the basics of how fasting works can create meaningful connection.

Try This Now: Boundary-Setting Practice

Establishing healthy boundaries around discussions of your fasting practice helps protect your emotional wellbeing while maintaining important relationships:

1. Identify a specific relationship or situation where discussing your fasting practice has been or might be challenging.
2. Write down what makes this particular interaction difficult (concern that feels like control, scepticism that feels dismissive, etc.).
3. Clarify your boundary goal—what specific limitation would make these interactions more comfortable? For example:
    a. Not discussing fasting details during family meals
    b. Redirecting conversation after briefly acknowledging questions
    c. Limiting fasting discussions to certain settings or times
    d. Requesting specific types of support rather than unsolicited advice
4. Craft a clear, kind boundary statement using this template: "I appreciate your [concern/interest/thoughts], and at the same time, I need [specific boundary]. Instead, I'd find it helpful if you [alternative supportive behaviour]."
5. Practice delivering this statement aloud several times, using a calm, confident tone.

6. Visualize yourself maintaining this boundary with compassionate firmness if initially met with resistance.

Example: "I appreciate your concern about my health, and at the same time, I need to make my own informed decisions about my eating patterns. Instead, I'd find it helpful if you could support me by not commenting on when or what I'm eating during family gatherings."

Regular practice with boundary-setting not only helps protect your fasting journey but often improves relationship dynamics across other areas of life as well.

Vulnerability and Sharing Your Journey

Deciding how openly to share your fasting practice involves navigating the tension between authentic connection and appropriate privacy. While sharing can create valuable support opportunities, it also opens you to opinions, judgment, and sometimes unwanted advice.

Balancing Connection and Protection

Consider these factors when deciding how much to share about your fasting journey:

Relationship Context: The nature and depth of specific relationships naturally affects appropriate sharing levels. Close supportive relationships often benefit from greater transparency than casual or professionally limited ones.

Personal Comfort: Your own comfort with vulnerability around health practices matters significantly. Some people find public accountability motivating; others experience it as added pressure.

Stage of Practice: Early in your fasting journey when you're still establishing patterns, more selective sharing often provides space to experiment without excessive external input.

Purpose of Sharing: Clarify why you're considering sharing—for support, accountability, to inspire others, or simply authentic connection. This purpose should guide both whom you tell and how much detail you provide.

Potential Impact: Consider how others might respond based on their own relationships with food, health, and body image. Sometimes limiting sharing protects not only you but others who might find fasting discussions triggering.

Sophia developed a thoughtful approach to sharing: "I'm completely open about my fasting practice with my husband and close friends who've shown genuine interest and support. With most colleagues and acquaintances, I simply don't bring it up, and if they notice I'm not eating at certain times, I keep explanations brief and change the subject. I've found being selective about where I direct my energy around explaining and defending my choices preserves that energy for actually maintaining my practice."

Creating Safe Spaces for Vulnerability

When you do choose to share your fasting journey with others, these practices can help create emotionally safer experiences:

Start with listening: Before sharing extensively about your practice, listen for cues about the other person's relationship with food and health changes. This context helps you frame your sharing appropriately.

Use "I" language: Framing your experience with "I" statements ("I've found this helpful for my energy" rather than "Fasting is the best way to improve energy") reduces defensiveness and respects different experiences.

Share struggles authentically: Discussing only successes creates incomplete connection. Thoughtfully sharing challenges demonstrates that you're approaching fasting realistically rather than idealistically.

Respect different choices: Explicitly acknowledging that different approaches work for different people creates space for connection even with those not practicing fasting.

Set information boundaries: Decide in advance which details of your practice you're comfortable discussing (general schedule, physical benefits) and which you prefer to keep private (weight changes, specific health concerns).

Invite specific support: Rather than leaving support undefined, request specific actions that would help you. "I'd love if you could suggest restaurant options that work well with my eating schedule" is clearer than general requests for support.

Safety and Support Checklist

Use this comprehensive checklist to ensure you've established necessary safety foundations and support structures for your fasting practice:

1. Consulted healthcare providers about how fasting might interact with your specific health conditions or medications.
2. Established baseline health metrics through appropriate tests or measurements before beginning fasting.
3. Identified specific symptoms or concerns that would prompt you to modify or pause your fasting practice.
4. Created an emergency plan for addressing significant discomfort or concerning symptoms during fasting periods.
5. Selected fasting approaches appropriate for your current health status and experience level.
6. Mapped your support network across different relationship categories.
7. Identified at least one person with whom you can discuss fasting experiences completely honestly.
8. Found credible online or in-person communities that align with evidence-based approaches to fasting.
9. Prepared responses for common questions or concerns others might raise about your fasting practice.
10. Established clear boundaries around discussing your eating patterns in potentially challenging relationships.

11. Developed strategies for social situations where food is central to the gathering.
12. Created methods to track both physical and emotional responses to your fasting practice.
13. Identified professional resources to consult if challenges arise beyond your current knowledge or peer support.
14. Scheduled regular reassessment points to review how your fasting practice is affecting your overall wellbeing.
15. Prepared flexibility strategies for adapting your fasting approach to changing life circumstances.

Creating Balance: Physical Safety and Emotional Wellbeing

As we conclude this chapter on safety and support, I want to emphasize that the most sustainable fasting practice honours both physical and emotional wellbeing as equally important considerations. Neither should be sacrificed for the other.

Physical safety without emotional wellbeing often leads to technically "correct" practices that feel joyless and unsustainable. Conversely, prioritizing emotional comfort while ignoring physical safety signals can lead to practices that feel good temporarily but potentially cause harm longer-term.

The balanced approach integrates appropriate caution, medical guidance when needed, strong social support, and personal boundaries—creating conditions where your fasting practice enhances rather than diminishes your overall quality of life.

Sophia reflected on this balance after two years of consistent practice: "In the beginning, I swung between extremes—pushing too hard and ignoring physical warning signs, then abandoning my practice entirely when that became unsustainable. What eventually worked was creating this middle path where I respect both my body's signals and my emotional needs. Some days that means a shorter fast because my body needs more support; other days it means maintaining my fasting window despite social pressure because I value how it makes me feel. This balanced approach has made fasting a sustainable part of my life rather than another health practice I tried and abandoned."

As you continue developing your fasting practice, regularly check in with both dimensions of your experience: Is this physically safe for my specific body and health situation? And does this approach support my emotional wellbeing and quality of life? When you can genuinely answer yes to both questions, you've found the sweet spot where fasting becomes not just another health practice but a sustainable lifestyle enhancer.

In our next chapter, we'll explore inspiring stories of real beginners who have successfully integrated intermittent fasting into their lives, overcoming challenges and experiencing multidimensional benefits that extend far beyond physical changes.

CHAPTER 9: SUCCESS STORIES: REAL BEGINNERS, REAL RESULTS

The Power of Shared Experience

There's something uniquely powerful about hearing from people who have walked the path ahead of you. While scientific evidence and practical guidance are essential foundations for your fasting practice, personal stories add a different kind of wisdom—the lived experience that illuminates both challenges and possibilities in ways that data alone cannot.

The stories in this chapter represent real journeys of people who began intermittent fasting as complete beginners. They span different ages, backgrounds, starting points, and motivations. While their specific experiences vary widely, each narrative contains elements you might recognize from your own life or anticipate on your path ahead.

As you read these stories, I invite you to look beyond the surface details to the deeper patterns and principles that made these individuals successful. Notice how they navigated challenges, the adjustments they made to personalize their approach, and the unexpected benefits they discovered beyond their initial goals. Their journeys offer not just inspiration but practical wisdom that you can apply to your own fasting practice.

Michael's Journey: From Prediabetic to Metabolically Healthy

At 53, Michael found himself at a health crossroads. A routine physical had revealed concerning news: his blood sugar had crept into the prediabetic range, his blood pressure required medication, and at 5'10" and 242 pounds, his doctor had bluntly suggested he needed to "do something" about his weight.

"That appointment was a wake-up call," Michael recalls. "I'd always seen myself as basically healthy despite carrying extra weight. I played recreational tennis, walked the dog, and didn't have any symptoms that bothered me. Finding out I was heading toward diabetes shocked me into reality."

Initial Scepticism and Research

Like many people, Michael's first instinct was to return to approaches he'd tried before—portion control, cutting out desserts, and adding more exercise. "I'd been on that merry-go-round many times," he admits. "Lose 15-20 pounds, get busy or stressed, gradually regain it plus a little more. I was honestly dreading another round of the same frustrating cycle."

It was Michael's sister who first mentioned intermittent fasting during a family dinner. "She'd been doing 16:8 fasting for about six months and couldn't stop talking about how much better she felt. But I was deeply sceptical. I'd always believed in the 'breakfast is the most important meal' idea and thought going without food for extended periods would make me irritable and unfocused."

Despite his doubts, Michael's concern about developing full-blown diabetes motivated him to research the approach. "What finally convinced me was finding actual medical research showing how fasting periods could improve insulin sensitivity. I'm an engineer—I need to understand mechanisms and see evidence before I try something."

Early Struggles with Hunger and Habits

Michael decided to start with a modest 12-hour overnight fast, essentially just stopping after dinner at 8pm and not eating until breakfast at 8am. "Even that was an adjustment since I'd been in the habit of late-night snacking while watching TV," he explains.

The first week presented several challenges. "The physical hunger wasn't actually as bad as I'd expected, but the habit disruption was tough. Around 9:30 each night, I'd get this powerful urge to head to the kitchen—not because my body needed food, but because that's what I'd always done during my favourite shows."

Michael developed a strategy for those difficult evening hours: herbal tea with a splash of milk (which he later eliminated as he learned more about clean fasting) and moving to a different chair than his usual TV-watching spot to disrupt the environmental cues for snacking.

Mornings presented their own challenges. "For the first two weeks, I felt foggy and a bit headachy until around

9am," he recalls. "I was seriously questioning whether this approach would work for me since I needed mental clarity for my job."

Adaptation and First Breakthroughs

By the third week, Michael began noticing significant changes. "The morning fog started lifting. In fact, I was experiencing mental clarity that actually surpassed my previous baseline. I'd have these incredibly productive morning hours where I'd knock out complex work that would have taken me much longer before."

Encouraged by these cognitive improvements, Michael gradually extended his fasting window to 14 hours, then 16, typically eating between noon and 8pm. "The hunger I'd anticipated never materialized in the way I'd feared. I'd feel hungry occasionally, but it wasn't the desperate, must-eat-immediately sensation I'd expected."

A significant breakthrough came about a month into his practice. "I had a weekend tennis match scheduled for 10am—right in the middle of my fasting period. I was concerned about having enough energy, but decided to try it without changing my eating schedule. Not only did I have plenty of energy, I felt more focused and light on my feet than usual. That's when I really started to trust that my body could function well without constant feeding."

Physical and Emotional Transformation

Over six months, Michael's body underwent significant changes. His weight decreased from 242 to 204 pounds, but more importantly to him, his metabolic health markers improved dramatically. "My fasting blood glucose went from 108 to 82, my blood pressure normalized to the point where my doctor reduced my medication, and my chronic knee pain diminished as the excess weight came off."

Beyond these physical changes, Michael experienced emotional and social transformations he hadn't anticipated. "My relationship with food changed fundamentally. I still enjoy eating, maybe even more than before, but food doesn't have the same control over me. I can be in situations with abundant food and feel completely comfortable choosing not to eat if it's during my fasting window."

This new relationship with food spilled over into his family dynamics as well. "My wife and I used to default to food-centred activities—trying new restaurants was our main weekend activity. While we still enjoy dining out, we've expanded our repertoire to include hiking, taking art classes together, and other experiences that aren't focused on consumption. Our relationship has actually deepened through these new shared activities."

Sustainable Integration

Now two years into his fasting practice, Michael has settled into a sustainable pattern that flexes with his life needs. "I typically follow a 16:8 schedule during the workweek, eating from noon to 8pm. On weekends, I'm more flexible—sometimes maintaining the same schedule, sometimes shortening my fasting window to join family for brunch, occasionally extending it if I'm particularly engaged in a project and don't notice hunger."

He no longer tracks his fasting hours precisely and describes his approach as "structured but not rigid." The health benefits have maintained even with this flexible approach—his weight has stabilized around 200 pounds, and his metabolic markers remain in healthy ranges.

"What surprised me most was how this became less about 'dieting' and more about discovering a way of eating that actually feels natural," Michael reflects. "I don't feel deprived or like I'm constantly exerting willpower. Most days, I simply don't get hungry until around noon, and stopping after dinner feels normal now."

Lessons Learned

From Michael's experience:

1. Initial scepticism can be healthy if it leads to research rather than dismissal. Understanding the mechanisms and evidence behind fasting created the foundation for Michael's committed practice.
2. Habit disruption often proves more challenging than physical hunger. Creating specific strategies for habitual eating times (like evening TV snacking) can be crucial for early success.
3. The adaptation period varies individually. For Michael, mental clarity took about three weeks to improve, which required patience through the initial foggy mornings.
4. Testing fasting in different contexts (like his

tennis match) built confidence in his body's capabilities and expanded what he thought possible.
5. Benefits beyond the original goal often become the most meaningful motivators. While Michael started fasting for blood sugar management, the mental clarity and improved relationship with food became equally important reasons to continue.
6. Flexibility increases with experience. As his practice matured, Michael moved from strict scheduling to a more intuitive approach that accommodates life's variables while maintaining core benefits.

Elena's Story: Finding Balance in a High-Pressure Career

At 34, Elena was thriving professionally as a marketing executive but feeling increasingly disconnected from her physical wellbeing. Long hours, frequent business meals, and stress-driven eating had created patterns that left her feeling constantly fatigued despite her career success.

"I was the classic 'work hard, play hard' professional," Elena explains. "Business dinners with clients multiple nights a week, team lunches, stress eating during deadlines, and grabbing whatever was convenient when I finally had a moment to breathe. I'd gained about 30 pounds over five years, but more concerning was how depleted I felt all the time."

The Breaking Point

Elena's wake-up call came during a particularly

demanding product launch. "I was in a key presentation and completely lost my train of thought mid-sentence. I stood there in front of the executive team, unable to remember what I was saying. I covered it decently, but that brain fog terrified me. I wondered if I was burning out or if something was seriously wrong with my health."

A visit to her doctor revealed nothing clinically concerning but confirmed that her lifestyle was taking a toll. "My doctor mentioned that my constant eating pattern—I literally never went more than 2-3 hours without food during waking hours—might be contributing to energy fluctuations and brain fog. She suggested I might benefit from longer periods between meals."

Confronting Fears and Finding Approach

When Elena first heard about intermittent fasting from a colleague, her immediate reaction was concern. "My biggest fear was that fasting would make me less effective at work. I couldn't afford any drop in performance, especially during client meetings or presentations. I was also worried about maintaining my social life, which revolved heavily around meals with friends and business contacts."

These concerns led Elena to approach fasting cautiously, starting with a modest 12-hour overnight fast and focusing initially on days when she had morning meetings where sharp thinking was essential. "I decided to test the mental clarity benefits I'd read about in a controlled way. I'd fast from 8pm until 10am, then evaluate how I felt during my morning meetings compared to days when I had breakfast."

Navigating Professional Challenges

The professional environment presented unique challenges for Elena's fasting practice. "Client breakfasts were a regular part of my schedule. I had to figure out how to handle those situations without making fasting the focus of attention or seeming difficult."

She developed several strategies to navigate these situations: "For breakfast meetings, I'd order black coffee and explain I was trying a new eating schedule if anyone asked. Most people were surprisingly uninterested in my eating habits. For lunch meetings, I'd schedule them for the later part of my day when I was eating. For dinner events, I'd adjust my eating window that day to accommodate the social aspect, which felt like a reasonable trade-off."

The most difficult situations were multi-day conferences and business trips. "Those environments are designed around constant food availability. I learned to bring fasting-friendly electrolyte supplements and to scope out quiet places where I could retreat during meal times if I was fasting."

Unexpected Professional Benefits

While Elena had feared fasting might hinder her career, she discovered the opposite effect. "The mental clarity I experienced during fasted mornings became my secret professional advantage. I started scheduling my most demanding cognitive work—strategic planning, creative development, complex problem-solving—

during my fasting hours when my thinking was sharpest."

This strategic use of her fasting-enhanced cognition led to notable career developments. "Six months in, I led a major strategy presentation that honestly represented some of my best work ever. The clarity and confidence I projected led to my promotion to senior director. I'm convinced that the cognitive benefits of fasting played a significant role in that advancement."

Beyond individual performance, Elena noticed changes in how she led her team. "I became more present and patient in team interactions. Without the energy crashes I used to experience, I could maintain consistent focus throughout day-long meetings and actually listen more effectively to my team members."

Physical and Emotional Evolution

While Elena's primary motivation had been energy and cognitive function, physical changes naturally followed. "I lost about 25 pounds over eight months without focusing on weight loss as a goal. More importantly, my energy became consistent throughout the day instead of the dramatic peaks and crashes I used to experience."

The emotional changes surprised her even more. "I had no idea how much of my eating was stress-driven until I created these fasting windows where eating simply wasn't an option. This forced me to develop other stress management techniques—brief meditation, short walks, even just conscious breathing—that actually addressed the stress rather than just temporarily distracting from it with food."

Elena also discovered unexpected emotional benefits in her relationship with hunger. "Learning that hunger wasn't an emergency that required immediate resolution was genuinely liberating. I'd spent years responding immediately to any hunger sensation, believing I needed to 'fuel up' constantly. Discovering I could feel hunger without acting on it immediately gave me a sense of freedom and control I hadn't expected."

Life Integration and Evolution

After a year of practice, Elena settled into a sustainable approach that accommodated her variable professional demands. "I typically follow a 16:8 schedule, eating between noon and 8pm on most days. However, I adjust this window based on my professional and social calendar rather than forcing my life to conform to rigid fasting times."

She's developed specific strategies for different professional scenarios:

1. Regular office days: 16:8 fasting (noon-8pm eating window)
2. Important morning presentation days: Maintained or even extended morning fast for peak cognitive performance
3. Client dinner evenings: Shifted eating window later (2-10pm) to accommodate evening obligations
4. Travel days: Modified to 14:10 to maintain basic benefits while allowing more flexibility

5. Multi-day conferences: Alternated between fasting days and more flexible eating days

"The key has been finding the balance between consistency and flexibility," Elena explains. "I maintain enough consistency to get the benefits but adapt when necessary for professional or personal reasons without feeling like I've 'failed' at fasting."

Lessons Learned

From Elena's experience:

1. Professional environments require strategic adaptation rather than rigid fasting schedules. Learning to navigate social eating situations diplomatically preserved important professional connections.
2. Cognitive benefits can be strategically leveraged by scheduling demanding mental tasks during peak fasting clarity periods.
3. Small explanations work better than detailed justifications. Elena found brief, matter-of-fact statements about her eating schedule avoided unnecessary attention or discussion.
4. Preparation prevents compromising situations, especially in environments designed around constant food availability like conferences and business travel.
5. Flexibility is not failure. Adapting fasting windows to accommodate important professional or social events supports sustainability without undermining overall benefits.
6. Alternative stress management techniques

become essential when food is no longer available as a coping mechanism during fasting periods.

Robert's Journey: Reclaiming Health in Later Life

At 67, Robert faced health challenges that were affecting his quality of life and independence. Retired from his career as a high school history teacher, he had hoped to spend his retirement years traveling, volunteering, and playing with his grandchildren. Instead, he found himself increasingly limited by joint pain, declining energy, and a growing list of medications.

"My doctor had been warning me for years about my weight and blood pressure, but I always found reasons to delay making changes," Robert explains. "It wasn't until I couldn't get down on the floor to play with my youngest grandchild that I realized how much my health was limiting the life I wanted to live."

Age-Related Concerns

When Robert's daughter suggested he consider intermittent fasting, his first reaction was skepticism tinged with concern. "At my age, I worried that fasting might be too extreme. I had the old-school belief that older people need to eat more frequently to maintain their strength. I was also concerned about how fasting might interact with my medications for blood pressure and cholesterol."

These concerns led Robert to consult his doctor before beginning. "I was surprised when my doctor was cautiously supportive after I explained the moderate approach I was considering. He suggested starting with a 12-hour overnight fast, continuing my medications as prescribed, and monitoring my blood pressure carefully."

Gentle Beginnings and Adaptation

Robert began with a simple overnight fast from 7pm to 7am, essentially just eliminating his evening snacking habit. "Even that modest change was challenging at first. I'd been in the habit of having cookies and milk while watching the evening news for decades. Breaking that pattern took real intention."

He developed a replacement routine to ease the transition: "I started having herbal tea in my favourite mug during the news instead. Having a warm drink gave me something to do with my hands and provided a different kind of comfort."

The initial adaptation brought expected challenges. "The first two weeks, I felt hungry in the evenings and a bit low on energy in the mornings. I worried this might be a sign that fasting wasn't appropriate for someone my age. But my doctor encouraged me to give it a full month before deciding."

Gradual Progress and Surprising Benefits

By the third week, Robert began noticing subtle improvements. "The first change I noticed wasn't weight-related at all—it was that I was sleeping better. For years, I'd been getting up 2-3 times each night to use the bathroom and often couldn't get back to sleep easily. Suddenly I was sleeping through until 5 or 6am without interruption."

This improved sleep quality led to better daytime energy, which encouraged Robert to gradually extend his fasting window. "Over about two months, I stretched my fasting period to 14 hours, typically from 6pm to 8am. This timing worked well with my natural patterns—I've always been an early dinner and early breakfast person."

The physical benefits accumulated gradually but significantly. Over six months, Robert lost 27 pounds, and his doctor was able to reduce both his blood pressure and cholesterol medications. Perhaps most meaningful to him was the reduction in joint pain. "The inflammation in my knees decreased enough that I could get down on the floor with my grandkids again—not easily, but I could do it. That simple ability meant the world to me."

Unexpected Cognitive Benefits

One benefit Robert hadn't anticipated was the effect on his cognitive sharpness. "As a retired teacher, I'd been concerned about maintaining my mental acuity. I'd noticed some normal age-related changes in my memory and processing speed. About four months into fasting, my wife commented that I seemed more mentally sharp—remembering names better and following complex discussions with greater ease."

This observation led Robert to add brain health to his motivations for continuing his fasting practice. "The research connecting fasting to brain health is particularly relevant at my age. The possibility that this practice might help preserve my cognitive function or even reduce risk of dementia became very motivating for me."

Family Dynamics and Social Adjustments

Robert's fasting practice required adjustments within his family routines. "My wife and I had to rework our dinner timing, moving it earlier so I could complete dinner by 6pm most days. She was supportive but didn't want to adopt fasting herself, so we had to find a balance that worked for both of us."

Social situations presented their own challenges. "Our generation's social life revolves heavily around meals, particularly dinner gatherings that tend to start later than my eating window. I had to decide how to handle those situations without becoming isolated."

Robert developed a flexible approach to social occasions. "For special events and gatherings with close friends, I adjust my schedule and accept that I might not get a full 14-hour fast that day. For regular social activities, we've started suggesting lunch gatherings instead of dinners when possible, which works better with my eating window."

Sustainable Practice for Longevity

Now eighteen months into his intermittent fasting practice, Robert has settled into a sustainable pattern that supports his health while accommodating the realities of retired life. "I maintain a 14-hour fast most days, essentially following a 8am to 6pm eating window. Once a week, I extend to 16 hours if I'm feeling good. On special occasions or family events, I adjust as needed without guilt."

The practices that support his fasting have become seamlessly integrated into his daily routine. "I take a morning walk before breakfast, which seems to set a positive tone for the day. I've found that having protein and healthy fat with my first meal keeps me satisfied longer. And herbal tea in the evening has completely replaced my old cookies-and-milk habit."

Robert's approach focuses on quality of life rather than strict adherence to specific fasting protocols. "At my age, my primary goal isn't weight loss or even longevity in the abstract—it's maintaining functional independence and enjoying the life I have. Fasting has become a tool that supports those goals rather than an end in itself."

Lessons Learned

From Robert's experience:

1. Medical consultation is particularly important for older adults and those taking medications. Robert's decision to involve his doctor from the beginning ensured his approach was safe and appropriate.
2. Starting gently with modest fasting windows allowed for gradual adaptation and confidence building, particularly important for older beginners.
3. Sleep quality improvements may be an early benefit that supports continuation through other adaptation challenges.
4. Social flexibility prevents isolation, especially in life stages where social connections often

centre around meals.
5. Cognitive benefits provide powerful motivation for maintaining fasting practices, particularly for those concerned about age-related cognitive changes.
6. Functional improvements often matter more than weight loss, especially in older adults. Robert's ability to play with his grandchildren provided more meaningful motivation than scale numbers.

Aisha's Experience: Integrating Fasting with Physical Demands

As a 29-year-old nurse working 12-hour shifts in a busy emergency department, Aisha faced unique challenges in establishing a sustainable fasting practice. Her work involved constant movement, unpredictable breaks, and the mental strain of critical decision-making—all factors that made her initially sceptical about restricting her eating window.

"In nursing school, we were taught to never skip meals during shifts because we needed steady energy for patient care," Aisha explains. "I'd developed the habit of grabbing quick snacks whenever possible during shifts, believing this was necessary to maintain my performance. I also used food as stress management during particularly difficult days."

Professional Concerns and Hesitation

When a colleague mentioned how intermittent fasting had improved her energy levels during night shifts, Aisha was intrigued but concerned. "My biggest worry was whether I could maintain the mental sharpness and physical stamina my job requires. I couldn't risk feeling faint while caring for patients or having delayed reactions during emergencies."

These legitimate concerns led Aisha to research carefully before attempting any changes. "I specifically looked for studies or accounts of people in physically and mentally demanding jobs who practiced fasting. I wanted to understand the adjustments they made and how they navigated challenges similar to mine."

After consulting with her primary care provider and reading accounts from other healthcare workers, Aisha decided to start with a modified approach specifically designed around her shift schedule rather than the standard 16:8 protocol.

Shift-Specific Adaptation

Rather than following a time-based fasting schedule, Aisha developed a shift-centred approach. "I realized trying to maintain the same eating window regardless of whether I was working day or night shifts would be nearly impossible and potentially unsafe. Instead, I organized my fasting around my shift pattern."

For day shifts (7am-7pm), she would:

1. Eat a substantial meal with protein, healthy fats, and complex carbohydrates before her shift
2. Bring a single nutrient-dense meal to eat approximately midway through her shift
3. Fast from the end of that meal until breakfast

the next morning

For night shifts (7pm-7am), she would:
1. Eat normally during the day before her shift
2. Have a balanced meal before reporting to work
3. Fast throughout the night shift, supported by water, electrolytes, and black coffee
4. Have a small protein-focused meal before sleeping in the morning

This approach created varying fasting windows ranging from 14-16 hours depending on her shift pattern, but always positioned her eating periods to support her work performance.

Early Challenges and Adjustments

The first month presented several challenges as Aisha's body adapted to her new eating pattern. "The night shifts were particularly difficult at first. Around 3-4am, I'd experience significant energy dips that made me question whether fasting was compatible with my work."

She made several key adjustments during this adaptation phase:

1. Added electrolytes to her water during fasting periods
2. Strategically timed caffeine consumption for the most challenging hours
3. Incorporated brief 5-minute movement breaks during energy dips
4. Kept emergency protein sources (like a small serving of nuts) available if patient care

demands required additional support

"The key realization was that I needed to distinguish between actual physical need for food and habitual stress eating," Aisha explains. "When I felt energy dips, I'd first try electrolytes, movement, or just deep breathing. If those didn't help within 15 minutes and I was caring for patients, I would have a small amount of nuts without considering it a 'failure' of my fasting plan."

Discovering Unexpected Advantages

After the initial adjustment period, Aisha began noticing significant benefits that specifically enhanced her nursing practice. "The most surprising benefit was improved focus during critical situations. Without the blood sugar fluctuations I used to experience, I found I could maintain clearer thinking during emergent cases."

She also discovered that fasting during shifts eliminated the post-meal energy dips that had previously affected her. "I used to feel sluggish after eating during shifts, especially during night shifts when digestion is naturally slower. Fasting during most of my shift eliminated that afternoon crash I used to push through."

An unexpected professional benefit emerged in her ability to better empathize with patients who were fasting for medical procedures. "I developed more authentic compassion for patients who couldn't eat before surgeries or procedures. Instead of just saying 'I know it's hard,' I could genuinely understand their experience and offer more helpful coping strategies."

Physical and Emotional Transformation

Beyond her professional performance, Aisha experienced significant personal health improvements. "I lost 18 pounds over about five months without feeling deprived, but more importantly, my energy became much more consistent both during and between shifts."

The emotional benefits proved equally valuable. "Nursing can be emotionally draining, and I'd developed the habit of using food to manage those feelings. Fasting periods forced me to develop other emotional regulation strategies—deep breathing, brief meditation during breaks, short walks, or connecting with colleagues. These approaches actually addressed the emotional weight of difficult cases better than stress eating ever did."

She also found that fasting improved her sleep quality between shifts, a critical factor for shift workers. "When I fast for several hours before sleep, particularly after night shifts, I fall asleep more easily and experience deeper rest. Given the sleep disruption inherent in shift work, this benefit alone would make fasting worthwhile for me."

Long-Term Integration with Shift Work

After eight months of practice, Aisha developed a sustainable approach that accommodated her rotating shift schedule while maintaining the benefits of intermittent fasting. "I no longer follow rigid rules but instead have flexible guidelines based on my shift pattern, physical needs, and social life."

Her typical patterns evolved to:

Day Shifts:
1. 14-16 hour fasts from evening until mid-shift the next day
2. One substantial meal during her 30-minute break
3. Flexibility to include a small protein serving if needed during particularly demanding shifts

Night Shifts:
1. 16-18 hour fasts during the shift and through morning sleep
2. Normal eating window during awake hours on days off

Days Off:
1. More typical 16:8 pattern (eating between 11am-7pm)
2. Adjustments for social occasions without guilt

"The beauty of this approach is how it adapts to the realities of my work rather than forcing rigid timing that might compromise patient care or my wellbeing," Aisha explains. "On particularly demanding shifts with multiple codes or traumas, I give myself permission to modify as needed, while maintaining the overall pattern that supports my health."

Lessons Learned

From Aisha's experience:

1. Safety-critical professions require thoughtful

fasting adaptation rather than adherence to standard protocols. Patient care and professional responsibilities always take precedence.
2. Shift-based rather than time-based fasting windows offer more sustainable approaches for those with variable work schedules.
3. Strategic placement of meals relative to high-demand periods can optimize both fasting benefits and work performance.
4. Electrolytes become particularly important during fasting periods with high physical demands or unpredictable environments.
5. Distinguishing between habitual and necessary eating develops with practice and body awareness.
6. Flexible guidelines work better than rigid rules for those whose work demands vary significantly from day to day.
7. Sleep quality benefits are especially valuable for shift workers and those with disrupted sleep patterns.

Common Patterns and Insights Across Diverse Experiences

While each individual's journey with intermittent fasting is unique, certain patterns and insights emerge across these diverse experiences:

The Adaptation Curve

Nearly all successful practitioners describe a similar adaptation pattern: initial challenges followed by a turning point where the practice becomes notably easier. This adaptation typically occurs within 2-4 weeks but varies based on individual factors and chosen fasting approach.

Understanding this curve helps beginners persist through initial difficulties with the knowledge that adaptation—not permanent struggle—lies ahead. As Michael noted, "If I'd judged fasting solely on my first week's experience, I would have missed all the benefits that came after my body adapted."

Personalization Proves Essential

Each success story highlights the importance of personalizing fasting approaches to individual circumstances rather than rigidly following prescriptive protocols. Whether adapting to shift work like Aisha, accommodating age-related concerns like Robert, navigating professional demands like Elena, or working with specific health issues like Michael, personalization consistently emerges as a key factor in long-term success.

This personalization typically evolves through experimentation, reflection, and growing body awareness rather than emerging fully-formed at the outset. As Elena observed, "My optimal approach after a year looks very different from where I started. That evolution through personal experience was necessary—no book or expert could have prescribed my perfect fasting pattern from day one."

Benefits Beyond Initial Goals

A striking pattern across diverse experiences is how practitioners often continue their fasting practice for benefits they didn't initially seek or expect. Michael began fasting for blood sugar management but continued largely for the mental clarity and improved relationship with food. Elena sought energy stability but discovered profound professional advantages and stress management tools. Robert's joint pain improvement and enhanced sleep became more motivating than his original weight loss goal.

This pattern suggests that approaching fasting with curiosity about your body's unique responses may reveal personalized benefits that become powerful motivators for continued practice.

Social Dimension Requires Strategic Navigation

Across various life circumstances, successfully integrating fasting into social contexts consistently requires thoughtful strategies rather than isolation or rigid adherence. Whether in professional settings like Elena's client meals, family contexts like Robert's dinner timing adjustments, or shift work environments like Aisha's break room challenges, sustainable practice involves finding workable compromises rather than social withdrawal.

Successful practitioners develop approaches that preserve important connections while maintaining the core benefits of their fasting practice—recognizing that perfect adherence to fasting schedules matters less than overall consistency and life integration.

Emotional and Cognitive Benefits Often Become Primary

While physical benefits typically motivate most

beginners to start fasting, the emotional and cognitive transformations frequently become equally or more valued over time. Mental clarity, emotional regulation, freedom from food preoccupation, and improved relationship with hunger emerge as profound benefits that extend beyond physical health.

As Aisha noted, "I expected weight loss and maybe better energy. I didn't expect fasting would change how I relate to stress, improve my clinical decision-making, or enhance my empathy with patients. These benefits affect every dimension of my life, not just my health."

Reader Reflection Guide: Connecting Stories to Your Journey

These success stories offer richest value when you connect them thoughtfully to your own circumstances and goals. Consider these reflection questions to help translate others' experiences into insights for your personal practice:

1. Which aspects of these stories resonate most strongly with your situation? Consider similarities in challenges, motivations, or life circumstances.
2. What specific strategies from these experiences might you adapt for your own practice? Look for approaches that address challenges similar to yours.
3. Which benefits described by these individuals would be most meaningful in your life? Consider which outcomes would most significantly enhance your wellbeing.
4. What concerns or obstacles in your situation

aren't addressed in these stories? Identifying these gaps can help you seek additional resources or support.
5. How might you need to personalize your approach based on your unique circumstances? Consider your health status, work demands, family situation, and personal preferences.
6. What timeline for adaptation seems realistic given your situation? Set expectations based on similarities between your starting point and those described in these stories.
7. Which support systems or accountability structures could help your journey? Consider what helped these individuals navigate challenges successfully.
8. What breakthrough moments can you watch for as indicators of progress? Identifying potential milestones can help maintain motivation through initial challenges.

Remember that these stories represent individual journeys—your experience will necessarily differ in specific ways while potentially following similar patterns. The value lies not in perfectly replicating another's path but in gathering insights that inform your unique journey.

As you continue reading practical guidance in the following chapters, keep these real experiences in mind. They provide context and human dimension to the more structured guidance ahead, reminding us that behind every fasting practice is a person navigating both challenges and discoveries on their path to enhanced wellbeing.

CHAPTER 10: YOUR COMPLETE 30-DAY BEGINNER'S PLAN

A Structure for Success, Not a Rigid Program

The 30-day plan you're about to discover isn't a rigid protocol that demands perfection. Think of it instead as a supportive framework—a carefully designed structure that guides your initial fasting journey while leaving room for personal adjustment and discovery. This approach acknowledges both the universal patterns of fasting adaptation and the beautiful uniqueness of your individual body and life circumstances.

Many beginners find that having a clear structure for their first month provides reassurance and direction during what can otherwise feel like uncertain territory. This plan gives you that structure while emphasizing flexibility and personal exploration—the balance that leads to sustainable practice rather than temporary adherence followed by abandonment.

Throughout this 30-day framework, you'll notice a progressive approach that honours your body's need for gradual adaptation. Rather than pushing immediately into extended fasting periods, we'll build your fasting muscle gradually, allowing your metabolism, hunger hormones, and daily habits to adjust at a reasonable pace. This gentle progression significantly increases your chances of creating a sustainable practice rather than an unsustainable challenge.

The plan includes not just fasting durations but also preparation strategies, mindset development, challenge navigation, and progress recognition beyond physical changes. This comprehensive approach addresses the full spectrum of your fasting experience rather than focusing exclusively on hours and schedules.

As you engage with this plan, remember that it serves you, not the other way around. While consistency builds the foundation for successful fasting, the occasional deviation or adjustment doesn't constitute failure—it represents thoughtful personalization and self-awareness. Your goal isn't perfect adherence to this plan but rather developing a sustainable relationship with fasting that enhances your overall wellbeing.

Before You Begin: Assessment and Preparation

Before embarking on your 30-day journey, taking time for thoughtful assessment and preparation creates a strong foundation for success. This preparation phase isn't just practical planning—it's also about creating the mental and emotional groundwork that supports sustainable practice.

Personal Readiness Assessment Tool

Take a few minutes to honestly assess your current starting point with this simple assessment:

Physical Readiness
1. Current energy levels (1-10 scale): _____
2. Sleep quality (1-10 scale): _____
3. Existing health conditions (list): _____
4. Current medications (list): _____
5. Typical hunger patterns (when/how intense): _____
6. Current eating schedule (typical timing): _____

Environmental Readiness
1. Supportive people in your life (list): _____
2. Potential challenges in your environment: _____
3. Access to fasting-friendly beverages: _____
4. Work/schedule considerations: _____
5. Social commitments in the next 30 days: _____

Mental/Emotional Readiness
1. Primary motivation for trying fasting: _____
2. Concerns or fears about fasting: _____
3. Previous experience with hunger: _____
4. Confidence in ability to implement changes (1-10): _____

5. Stress level (1-10): _____
6. Relationship with food (describe briefly): _____

This assessment isn't about qualifying or disqualifying yourself for fasting—it's about honestly acknowledging your starting point so you can make appropriate adjustments to the general framework. For example, if your stress level is currently very high, you might choose to start with shorter fasting periods. If you have limited support, you might prioritize finding online communities before beginning.

Medical Consideration Reminder

Before proceeding, ensure you've addressed any necessary medical considerations:

▫ Consulted healthcare provider if you have existing health conditions ▫ Discussed medication timing with prescribing provider if relevant ▫ Received appropriate baseline measurements if tracking health markers ▫ Identified any personal contraindications that require modification ▫ Developed plan for monitoring any health concerns during fasting

Remember that this 30-day plan assumes generally good health with no major contraindications to fasting. If you have specific health considerations, work with your healthcare provider to modify this approach appropriately for your situation.

Preparation Checklist

Setting up your environment and mindset before beginning significantly increases your chances of success. Complete these preparations before Day 1:

1. Stock fasting-friendly beverages – water, herbal teas, black coffee, electrolyte supplements without calories
2. Prepare your kitchen – organize nutritious foods for eating windows, consider temporarily removing major temptation foods during initial adaptation
3. Set up tracking method – choose a journal, app, or calendar for monitoring your fasting periods and experiences
4. Create a support plan – identify at least one person or community you can turn to for encouragement
5. Establish success metrics – decide which indicators beyond weight will help you recognize progress
6. Schedule your fasting windows – review your calendar for the next 30 days and identify any events requiring adjustment
7. Plan your first week's meals – ensure you have nourishing foods available for your eating windows
8. Create contingency strategies – decide in advance how you'll handle specific challenges like unexpected hunger or social pressure
9. Set calendar reminders – schedule weekly check-ins to reflect on your experience
10. Establish your mindset – approach this as an experiment and learning experience rather than a test of willpower
11. Take baseline measurements – record starting

weight if relevant, along with energy levels, sleep quality, and other metrics important to you

Taking time to complete these preparations transforms your 30-day plan from an abstract intention into a concrete, supported practice ready for implementation.

Your 30-Day Roadmap: The Progressive Journey

Here's a visual overview of how your fasting practice will evolve over the next 30 days:

Phase 1: Days 1-7 – First Steps and Initial Adaptation

Focus: Establishing baseline fasting comfort Typical Window: 12-hour overnight fast Key Milestones: Completing first successful fasts, noticing initial hunger patterns

Phase 2: Days 8-14 – Building Consistency and Stability

Focus: Extending fasting window gradually Typical Window: Working toward 14-hour fasts Key Milestones: First experience of hunger waves passing, morning energy improvement

Phase 3: Days 15-21 – Deepening Practice and Awareness

Focus: Refining approach and noticing benefits Typical Window: 14-16 hour fasts based on individual adaptation Key Milestones: Mental clarity experiences, decreased hunger urgency

Phase 4: Days 22-30 – Personalization and Integration

Focus: Adapting practice to your unique needs Typical

Window: Personalized based on experience (typically 14-18 hours) Key Milestones: Confident navigation of challenges, intuitive adjustments

This progressive approach honours your body's need for adaptation while steadily building your fasting capacity. The specific timing windows are guidelines rather than rigid requirements—your personal experience may indicate faster or slower progression based on your unique response.

Phase 1: Days 1-7 – First Steps and Initial Adaptation

The first week focuses on establishing a baseline 12-hour overnight fast, which creates a natural break between dinner and breakfast without requiring significant schedule adjustments for most people. This gentle introduction allows your body to begin adapting to defined fasting periods while minimizing discomfort.

What to Expect Physically

During this first week, physical experiences typically include:

Hunger Patterns: You'll likely notice hunger arising at your usual eating times, particularly if you've been accustomed to evening snacking. This hunger often feels more urgent than it will in later weeks as your body still expects food on its habitual schedule.

Energy Fluctuations: Some people experience mild energy dips, particularly in the morning hours if they were previously breakfast eaters. These fluctuations are normal as your metabolism begins adapting to accessing stored energy.

Digestive Changes: You may notice changes in digestion or bowel movements as your digestive system adjusts to longer overnight rest periods. These changes are typically temporary as your system adapts.

Sleep Effects: Many people notice improved sleep quality even in this first week, though some initially experience disrupted sleep that improves with continued practice.

Thirst Signals: As you become more attentive to body sensations, you may notice increased thirst, particularly upon waking. This represents improved awareness rather than new dehydration.

What to Expect Emotionally

The emotional journey during week one often includes:

Initial Enthusiasm: Most beginners start with excitement and motivation to experience the benefits they've heard about or read about.

Uncertainty and Doubt: As initial challenges arise, moments of doubt are normal—questioning whether this approach is right for you or whether you can successfully implement it.

Heightened Food Awareness: Many notice increased attention to food thoughts during fasting periods, which can feel uncomfortable but represents growing awareness of habitual patterns.

Accomplishment: Successfully completing your first intentional fasting periods, even short ones, often brings a sense of achievement and competence.

Curiosity: As physical sensations arise during fasting periods, many experience growing curiosity about their body's signals and patterns.

Daily Guidance for Week One

Day 1: Focus simply on completing a 12-hour overnight fast, from dinner until breakfast the following day. Choose a 12-hour window that aligns with your natural sleep period, such as 7pm to 7am or 8pm to 8am. During your eating window, eat normally—this week isn't about changing what you eat, just when you eat.

Keep your first day simple and celebrate successfully completing your first intentional fasting period, even if 12 hours feels easy. Notice any habitual evening snacking urges without judgment.

Day 2: Maintain the same 12-hour overnight fast, perhaps slightly refined based on your Day 1 experience. Begin paying attention to hunger sensations—when they arise, their intensity, and how they change over time.

Notice the difference between actual physical hunger (empty feeling in stomach, mild hollow sensation) versus habitual eating urges (triggered by time, activities, or emotions but without physical symptoms).

Day 3: Continue the 12-hour pattern, adding mindfulness to your first meal when breaking your fast. Eat this meal slowly and attentively, noticing flavours and satisfaction levels. This day often presents the first notable challenge as initial novelty diminishes.

Pay particular attention to hydration throughout the day, as proper fluid intake significantly improves the fasting experience. Consider adding a pinch of salt to your morning water for electrolyte support.

Day 4: Maintain the 12-hour fasting window, adding awareness of your energy patterns throughout the day. Note times when you feel most energetic and focused versus periods of lower energy.

Begin connecting these energy patterns to your eating timing—many notice energy fluctuations after certain meals or during specific fasting periods. This awareness builds foundation for future optimization.

Day 5: If your 12-hour fasts have felt manageable, experiment with extending to 13 hours for this day only. If 12 hours still feels challenging, maintain that window while focusing on improved hydration and electrolyte balance.

Pay attention to morning hunger levels—some begin noticing decreased morning hunger as their bodies adapt to the overnight fasting period.

Day 6: Return to the 12-hour window, focusing on the quality of your first meal after fasting. Ensure this meal contains adequate protein, healthy fats, and fibre to maintain satisfaction throughout your eating window.

Notice how different breaking-fast meals affect your energy and satisfaction. This awareness helps optimize your eating window in future weeks.

Day 7: Complete your week with a 12-hour fast, then take time for reflection on your first week's experience. Review your notes on hunger patterns, energy fluctuations, and overall experience.

Consider whether you feel ready to extend your fasting window in the coming week or whether more time at 12 hours would be beneficial for continued adaptation.

Common Challenges and Solutions for Week One

Challenge: Evening Hunger and Habitual Snacking *If you experience strong urges to eat during your evening fasting period...*

1. Prepare herbal tea or sparkling water as an alternative evening ritual
2. Plan engaging activities during usual snacking times
3. Notice whether hunger occurs while watching TV or other trigger activities
4. Remember that this adaptation challenge typically improves significantly within 5-10 days

Challenge: Morning Fatigue or Headaches *If you experience low energy or headaches upon waking or during morning hours...*

1. Ensure adequate hydration immediately upon waking
2. Add a pinch of high-quality salt to your morning water
3. Consider whether caffeine timing or consumption patterns need adjustment

4. If symptoms are significant, consider breaking your fast slightly earlier until better adapted

Challenge: Difficulty Sleeping *If your fasting practice seems to affect your sleep quality...*

   1. Ensure your last meal contains some complex carbohydrates
   2. Consider moving your eating window earlier so dinner isn't immediately before bed
   3. Try a caffeine curfew, avoiding caffeine at least 8 hours before bedtime
   4. Practice relaxation techniques before sleep to reduce potential hunger awareness

Challenge: Social Pressure or Comments *If others notice and question your changed eating pattern...*

   1. Prepare simple, non-defensive responses about your personal health experiment
   2. Avoid detailed explanations or justifications unless genuinely interested questions arise
   3. Remember that your health choices don't require others' approval or understanding
   4. Consider which relationships merit more detailed explanation versus casual inquiries

Success Indicators Beyond the Scale

During this first week, look for these early indicators of successful adaptation:

☐ Completing planned fasting periods, even if challenging ☐ Noticing decreased evening hunger by end of week ☐ Developing increased awareness of true hunger versus habitual eating ☐ Sleeping through the night more consistently ☐ Feeling slight improvements in morning energy ☐ Successfully navigating minor social challenges around eating timing ☐ Growing curiosity about your body's signals and patterns

Reflection Questions for Week One

Take time at week's end to consider these questions:

1. What was easier about this first week than I expected?
2. What was more challenging than I anticipated?
3. When during the day do I notice the strongest hunger sensations?
4. How has my sleep been affected, if at all?
5. What strategies helped me most when experiencing hunger?
6. What am I noticing about my energy patterns throughout the day?
7. How confident do I feel about continuing and potentially extending my fasting window?
8. What adjustments would make my practice more sustainable next week?

Phase 2: Days 8-14 – Building Consistency and Addressing Challenges

The second week focuses on gradually extending your fasting window while building consistency in your practice. For most people, this means working toward a 14-hour fast, typically by extending the morning fasting period rather than pushing the evening boundary significantly later.

What to Expect Physically

As your body continues adapting during week two, you may notice:

Changing Hunger Patterns: Many experience decreased morning hunger intensity as their bodies adapt to accessing stored energy. Hunger often becomes less urgent and more wavelike.

Improved Energy Stability: Energy fluctuations typically begin stabilizing, with fewer dramatic dips and more consistent energy, particularly during fasting periods.

Enhanced Morning Clarity: Many notice improved mental sharpness during morning fasting hours—a sign that your brain is becoming more efficient at utilizing ketones.

Digestive Regulation: Initial digestive adjustments usually stabilize during this week as your system adapts to your new eating pattern.

Changing Taste Perception: Some notice enhanced taste sensitivity, with food flavours becoming more pronounced and satisfying when breaking their fast.

What to Expect Emotionally

The emotional journey often shifts during week two:

Growing Confidence: Successfully completing your first week builds belief in your ability to maintain this practice despite challenges.

Decreased Food Preoccupation: Many notice they're

spending less mental energy thinking about food during fasting periods as the practice becomes more normalized.

Occasional Frustration: Despite overall progress, challenging days still occur and can feel discouraging. These temporary setbacks are normal and don't indicate failure.

Increased Body Trust: As you experience your body's adaptation, many develop greater trust in their body's capabilities and signals.

Curiosity About Extension: Successfully maintaining 12-hour fasts often naturally creates interest in exploring longer fasting periods.

Daily Guidance for Week Two

Day 8: Begin this week by extending your fasting window to 13 hours if you haven't already. For most people, extending the morning end of the fast (delaying breakfast) feels more natural than pushing the evening starting time later.

Pay close attention to how this small extension affects your hunger and energy. Notice whether your body adapts quickly or whether the additional hour feels challenging.

Day 9: Maintain the 13-hour fasting window, focusing particularly on your hydration strategy during fasting hours. Experiment with different fasting-friendly beverages—perhaps black coffee, various herbal teas, or sparkling water—to discover what best supports your fasting experience.

Begin noticing the quality of hunger—whether it comes in waves that pass or feels constant, and how it differs from your first-week experience.

Day 10: Continue with 13-hour fasts, adding awareness of your breaking-fast meal composition. Experiment with a protein-focused meal and notice how it affects your satiety and energy compared to a carbohydrate-heavy meal.

This is often when the first significant adaptations become noticeable—pay attention to any changes in your hunger patterns or energy compared to your first week.

Day 11: If your 13-hour fasts have felt manageable, experiment with extending to 14 hours for today only. If 13 hours still feels challenging, maintain that window while focusing on optimal hydration and fasting-window beverages.

Notice how your body responds to either maintenance or extension—this individual feedback guides your ideal progression pace.

Day 12: Return to a 13-hour fast regardless of yesterday's experiment, focusing on the emotional experience of fasting. Notice any patterns in your mood during fasted versus fed states.

Many begin experiencing enhanced mental clarity during longer fasting periods around this day—pay attention to any cognitive improvements you might notice.

Day 13: Based on your experience so far, choose either a 13 or 14-hour fast for today. Whichever you choose, pay special attention to breaking your fast mindfully rather than rushing to eat immediately when your window begins.

Notice how your hunger manifests immediately before breaking your fast compared to week one—many find it becomes less urgent even when present.

Day 14: Complete your second week with your chosen fasting duration (13-14 hours), then take time for reflection on your two-week experience. Review your notes on changing patterns, challenges, and improvements.

Consider your readiness to maintain a 14-hour fast consistently in the coming week, or whether more time at your current duration would be beneficial.

Common Challenges and Solutions for Week Two

Challenge: Plateauing Motivation *If your initial enthusiasm diminishes as fasting becomes routine...*

1. Connect with your deeper motivation beyond initial curiosity
2. Note non-scale benefits you're experiencing in a journal
3. Join online communities for fresh inspiration and perspectives
4. Create small challenges or experiments within your practice to maintain engagement

Challenge: Social Situations Arising *If social events*

conflict with your fasting schedule...

1. For special occasions, consider adjusting your fasting window rather than missing important connections
2. Prepare simple explanations for declining food during fasting periods
3. Suggest activities not centred around meals during your fasting hours
4. Practice confident body language when explaining your choices

Challenge: Weekend Disruption *If weekend schedules or activities disrupt your fasting pattern...*

1. Decide in advance whether to maintain identical timing or adjust for weekends
2. If adjusting, maintain the same fasting duration even if timing shifts
3. Create weekend-specific strategies for common challenges like brunch or late dinners
4. Remember that consistency across weeks matters more than perfect adherence every day

Challenge: Hunger Intensification When Extending Duration *If extending from 12 to 14 hours creates significant additional hunger...*

1. Extend gradually in 30-minute increments rather than adding full hours
2. Ensure adequate protein and healthy fats during your eating window
3. Strategic timing of black coffee or tea can help manage hunger during extension

4. Remember that hunger adaptation typically requires 3-5 days at the new duration

Success Indicators Beyond the Scale

During this second week, look for these indicators of successful adaptation:

▢ Decreased urgency of morning hunger sensations ▢ Successfully extending fasting duration, even if gradually ▢ First experiences of improved mental clarity during fasting ▢ Growing confidence in your ability to navigate hunger ▢ More stable energy throughout the day ▢ Reduced preoccupation with food during fasting periods ▢ Successfully navigating minor disruptions to your schedule ▢ Noticing individual patterns in your optimal fasting approach

Reflection Questions for Week Two

Take time at week's end to consider these questions:

1. How has my hunger changed from week one to week two?
2. What patterns am I noticing about when I feel most energetic during the day?
3. How has extending my fasting window affected my physical and emotional experience?
4. What challenges arose this week, and how did I navigate them?
5. What strategies have been most helpful for making fasting sustainable?
6. How has my sleep quality changed since beginning fasting?

7. What am I noticing about my relationship with food during eating windows?
8. What adjustments would support my practice becoming more sustainable?

Phase 3: Days 15-21 – Deepening Practice and Noticing Benefits

The third week focuses on consolidating your practice at 14 hours and potentially extending to 16 hours if your body is adapting well. This week typically brings more noticeable benefits as adaptation progresses, providing reinforcement for your continuing practice.

What to Expect Physically

As your body adaptation advances during week three, you may experience:

Metabolic Flexibility Improvements: Many notice significantly improved ability to transition between fasted and fed states without energy crashes or urgent hunger.

Enhanced Mental Clarity: The cognitive benefits often become more pronounced, with notable mental sharpness during fasting periods, particularly in the morning hours.

Decreased Hunger Intensity: Hunger usually becomes less demanding and more informational—a sensation you notice without feeling controlled by it.

Improved Digestion: Many report less bloating, more comfortable digestion, and more regular bowel patterns as their digestive system adapts to consistent fasting periods.

Changing Body Composition: Some begin noticing changes in how clothes fit or body measurements, even if scale weight changes remain modest.

Stable Energy Throughout Day: Energy levels typically become more consistent without the significant post-meal dips that were previously normal.

What to Expect Emotionally

The emotional journey often deepens during week three:

Growing Body Trust: Successfully navigating hunger and energy fluctuations builds confidence in your body's natural wisdom and capabilities.

Identity Shift: Many begin seeing themselves as "someone who fasts" rather than someone trying out fasting—a subtle but important identity evolution.

Decreased Food Fixation: Food often occupies less mental space even during eating windows, creating psychological freedom.

Increased Awareness of Non-Scale Benefits: Many begin noticing and appreciating benefits beyond weight—sleep quality, mental clarity, emotional stability, and simplified relationship with food.

Greater Curiosity About Body Signals: The growing awareness of hunger patterns, energy fluctuations, and mood connections often creates fascination with your body's communications.

Daily Guidance for Week Three

Day 15: Begin your third week by establishing a consistent 14-hour fast if you haven't already. Focus particularly on the first hour after your fasting window ends—practice breaking your fast mindfully with a nutritionally complete meal rather than rushed eating.

Notice how the quality of your fast-breaking meal affects your satisfaction and energy for subsequent hours. This awareness helps optimize your eating window.

Day 16: Maintain your 14-hour fast, adding specific attention to your physical activity during fasting periods. If you exercise, experiment with light movement during your fasted state and notice how it affects your energy and hunger.

Many find that light activity during fasting actually improves their experience by stabilizing energy and reducing hunger perception. Others prefer to exercise during their eating window. Notice your personal pattern.

Day 17: Continue with 14-hour fasting, focusing today on the cognitive effects you experience during your fasting period. Notice times of peak mental clarity and any changes in focus, creativity, or problem-solving ability.

This awareness helps you strategically schedule cognitive tasks to align with your periods of greatest mental sharpness—often during the latter part of your fasting window.

Day 18: If your 14-hour fasts have felt comfortable for several days, experiment with extending to 15 hours for today only. If 14 hours still feels challenging, maintain that window while focusing on optimizing your eating window nutrition.

Pay attention to hunger sensations during the extended hour if you choose this experiment. For many, hunger during extension feels less intense than expected as their body adapts to accessing stored energy.

Day 19: Return to 14-hour fasting regardless of yesterday's experiment. Today, focus on your emotional experience around eating and fasting. Notice any patterns in how your mood correlates with fasting duration, breaking your fast, or specific foods.

This emotional awareness helps distinguish between physical hunger and emotional eating triggers—a key distinction for sustainable practice.

Day 20: Based on your experience so far, choose either a 14, 15, or 16-hour fast for today. Whichever you choose, pay special attention to how your energy flows throughout the day and how it relates to your fasting and eating windows.

Many discover their optimal fasting duration by noticing when they naturally feel most energetic and focused. This personal feedback proves more valuable than following prescriptive schedules.

Day 21: Complete your third week with your chosen fasting duration, then take time for comprehensive reflection on your three-week experience. Review your notes on physical changes, emotional patterns, and overall wellbeing.

Consider whether you feel ready to establish a consistent 16-hour fast in the coming week or whether more time at your current duration would be beneficial. Remember that longer isn't always better—optimal duration varies by individual.

Common Challenges and Solutions for Week Three

Challenge: Social Pressure to Abandon Practice *If friends or family question your continuing practice...*

1. Clearly communicate the benefits you're personally experiencing rather than debating general fasting merits
2. Set boundaries around discussions of your eating patterns when necessary
3. Connect with like-minded individuals who understand and support your practice
4. Remember that your health choices don't require external validation

Challenge: Fasting Window Boredom *If your fasting routine starts feeling monotonous...*

1. Experiment with different fasting-friendly beverages to add variety
2. Create meaningful morning rituals that you enjoy during fasting hours
3. Vary your fast-breaking meals to maintain interest and nutritional diversity
4. Focus on the growing benefits rather than the temporary restriction

Challenge: Hunger Regression *If hunger temporarily intensifies after previous improvement...*

1. Remember that progress isn't always linear—temporary regression is normal
2. Check whether stress, poor sleep, or menstrual cycles might be affecting hunger
3. Ensure adequate protein and healthy fats during eating windows
4. Return temporarily to a shorter fasting window if needed, then gradually extend again

Challenge: Impatience for Results *If visible results seem slower than expected...*

1. Redirect attention to non-scale benefits you're experiencing
2. Document changes in measurements, photos, or clothing fit beyond scale weight
3. Remember that metabolic healing often precedes visible changes
4. Review your success indicators to recognize progress you might be overlooking

Success Indicators Beyond the Scale

During this third week, look for these indicators of deeper adaptation:

☐ Comfortable completion of 14-hour fasts ☐ Noticeable periods of mental clarity during fasting windows ☐ Decreased urgency when hunger arises ☐ More intuitive eating during your eating window ☐ Improved sleep quality and waking energy ☐ Successfully managing schedule variations without abandoning practice ☐

Reduced emotional attachment to eating at specific times ▫ Growing awareness of your unique optimal fasting pattern

Reflection Questions for Week Three

Take time at week's end to consider these questions:

1. What benefits am I now experiencing that I didn't notice in earlier weeks?
2. How has my experience of hunger continued to evolve?
3. What cognitive or emotional changes have I noticed during fasting periods?
4. How has my relationship with food shifted during eating windows?
5. What patterns am I discovering about my unique fasting response?
6. Which aspects of fasting have become easier, and which remain challenging?
7. How might I optimize my eating window nutrition to better support my fasting periods?
8. What would make this practice sustainable for me long-term?

Phase 4: Days 22-30 – Refinement and Personalization

The final phase of your 30-day journey focuses on refining your approach based on accumulated experience and creating a personalized practice that truly serves your unique body and lifestyle. This week emphasizes experimentation, reflection, and establishing sustainable patterns for continued practice beyond the initial 30 days.

What to Expect Physically

As your practice matures during this final phase, you may experience:

Stabilized Adaptation: Physical adaptation typically reaches a stable point where fasting feels comfortable and natural rather than challenging.

Individual Pattern Recognition: Your body's unique rhythms become more apparent, helping you identify your optimal fasting duration and timing.

Intuitive Hunger and Fullness: Many notice more reliable hunger and satiety signals during eating windows as hormonal balance improves.

Enhanced Recovery: Physical resilience often improves, with better recovery from exercise and less susceptibility to minor illnesses.

Sleep Optimization: Sleep quality typically reaches a new baseline, with more consistent rest and refreshed waking.

Natural Weight Stabilization: If weight loss was a goal, many notice a natural approach toward a healthy equilibrium without extreme fluctuations.

What to Expect Emotionally

The emotional journey often matures significantly during this phase:

Fasting Identity Integration: The practice typically shifts from something you're trying to an integrated part of your lifestyle and self-concept.

Food Freedom: Many experience profound liberation from food preoccupation, with meal timing becoming practical rather than emotionally charged.

Confidence in Adaptation: Successfully navigating various challenges builds trust in your ability to adapt your practice to different circumstances.

Balanced Perspective: The extremes of rigid adherence versus abandonment typically evolve into balanced flexibility based on body wisdom.

Future Curiosity: Many develop interest in how their practice might continue evolving and deepening beyond the initial 30 days.

Daily Guidance for Final Phase

Day 22: Begin this final phase by establishing your preferred fasting window based on your experience so far. For most people, this falls between 14-16 hours, but your personal adaptation should guide this choice rather than external standards.

Focus today on creating a consistent opening ritual for your eating window—a mindful practice that helps you transition intentionally from fasted to fed states rather than rushing into eating.

Day 23: Maintain your chosen fasting duration while experimenting with nutrition composition during your eating window. Test how different macronutrient balances affect your subsequent fasting experience.

Many discover that adequate protein and healthy fats significantly improve their next-day fasting comfort.

Notice your personal response to different nutritional approaches.

Day 24: Continue your established fasting duration while practicing flexibility with timing. If you've been rigid about exact times, experiment with shifting your window slightly earlier or later based on your day's demands.

This flexibility practice helps develop the adaptability needed for sustainable long-term practice amid life's variable schedules.

Day 25: Maintain your core fasting duration while experimenting with different fasting-window activities. Try meditation, light movement, creative work, or social connection during hours when you previously might have been eating.

These experiments help establish fasting not as absence of eating but as space for other meaningful activities and experiences.

Day 26: Practice your established fasting approach while focusing specifically on hunger awareness. When hunger arises, practice the pause—30-60 seconds of simply observing the sensation with curiosity before deciding whether or how to respond.

This growing space between sensation and response builds the emotional regulation that supports sustainable practice.

Day 27: Maintain your core fasting practice while discussing your experience with someone supportive—either someone from your personal life or in an online community. Articulating your journey often reveals insights and patterns you hadn't previously recognized.

This sharing also helps solidify your understanding and integration of the practice beyond the initial 30-day structure.

Day 28: Continue your established fasting approach while creating a contingency plan for various circumstances you might encounter going forward—travel, illness, high-stress periods, special celebrations, etc.

This advance planning transforms these situations from potential derailments into anticipated variations within your sustainable practice.

Day 29: Maintain your fasting practice while reflecting on the complete journey from day 1 to now. Notice changes in physical sensations, emotional responses, and overall relationship with fasting and food.

Begin considering how you'll approach your practice beyond the structured 30-day introduction—what elements you'll maintain, what you might adjust, and how you'll continue learning and refining.

Day 30: Complete your 30-day journey with your established fasting practice, then take time for comprehensive reflection and forward planning. Acknowledge both challenges overcome and benefits gained, and set intentions for your continued practice.

Remember that day 30 represents not an endpoint but a transition from structured introduction to personalized ongoing practice.

Common Challenges and Solutions for Final Phase

Challenge: Overthinking Optimization *If you find yourself excessively analysing every aspect of your practice...*

1. Remember that good enough is often better than perfect for sustainability
2. Focus on overall consistency rather than daily perfection
3. Trust your body's feedback over external prescriptions or tracking
4. Periodically practice "intuitive fasting" without rigid time monitoring

Challenge: Concern About Continuing Solo *If you're worried about maintaining practice without daily guidance...*

1. Connect with ongoing support communities (online forums, local groups, etc.)
2. Schedule regular personal check-ins to reflect on your experience
3. Create accountability with a like-minded friend or family member
4. Remember the body awareness and skills you've developed during these 30 days

Challenge: Special Event Navigation *If approaching celebrations or special events cause concern...*

1. Decide in advance which events warrant fasting adjustment and which don't
2. Create event-specific strategies that honour both your practice and the occasion

3. Remember that occasional flexibility strengthens rather than weakens your practice
4. Focus on returning to your core pattern after the event rather than perfectionism

Challenge: Progress Plateaus *If visible changes seem to slow or stall...*

1. Remind yourself that many benefits continue accruing beneath visible markers
2. Consider whether your current fasting approach has become your new healthy baseline
3. Experiment with minor variations in timing or eating window nutrition
4. Return focus to non-scale benefits that enhance quality of life regardless of visible changes

Emotional Milestones to Celebrate

Take time to acknowledge these significant developments that may have emerged during your 30-day journey:

☐ Hunger Confidence: The ability to experience hunger without anxiety or immediate response ☐ Food Freedom: Decreased preoccupation with food and eating during daily life ☐ Schedule Flexibility: Capacity to adjust timing without abandoning core practice ☐ Body Trust: Improved confidence in your body's signals and capabilities ☐ Identity Evolution: Shift from "trying fasting" to integrating fasting as part of your lifestyle ☐ Emotional Regulation: Enhanced ability to distinguish between emotional and physical hunger ☐

Mindful Eating: More attentive, satisfying relationship with food during eating windows □ Adaptive Capability: Confidence in navigating various life circumstances while maintaining practice

Month 1 Reflection Guide

As you complete your first month, take time for comprehensive reflection with these questions:

1. How has my physical experience of fasting changed from week 1 to week 4?
2. What emotional shifts have I noticed in my relationship with food and hunger?
3. Which aspects of fasting have become easier than I expected?
4. What challenges remain that I want to address in the coming month?
5. What benefits have I experienced beyond initial expectations?
6. How has fasting affected other areas of my life (sleep, energy, mood, focus, etc.)?
7. What have I learned about my body's unique patterns and needs?
8. What support structures would help me maintain this practice long-term?
9. How might I continue personalizing my approach in the coming months?
10. What am I most proud of accomplishing during these 30 days?

Planning Your Continued Journey

As you transition from this structured 30-day introduction to ongoing practice, consider these planning elements for sustainable continuation:

Assessment of Your Ideal Approach

Based on your month-long experience, define your personal fasting framework:

Your Optimal Fasting Duration: The window that balances benefits with sustainability for your body Your Preferred Timing: The schedule that works best with your natural rhythms and life demands Your Weekday/Weekend Balance: How consistent or variable your approach will be across the week Your Special Occasion Strategy: How you'll handle celebrations, travel, and unusual circumstances Your Support System: The people, communities, or resources that will sustain your practice

Creating Sustainable Structures

Establish simple structures that support your continued practice:

☐ Regular Reassessment Points: Schedule monthly check-ins to reflect on your experience ☐ Minimal Effective Tracking: Determine the simplest monitoring that supports consistency ☐ Environmental Supports: Organize your physical environment to facilitate your practice ☐ Social Communication: Clarify how you'll discuss your practice with various people in your life ☐ Learning Plan: Identify resources for continued education about fasting as questions arise ☐ Adaptation Strategy: Establish how you'll adjust your approach during illness, travel, or high stress

Balanced Expectations Moving Forward

As you continue beyond day 30, maintain these perspective elements:

1. **Progress Continues Non-Linearly:** Expect ongoing adaptation with both improvements and occasional setbacks
2. **Benefits Often Deepen Subtly:** Some of the most valuable changes emerge gradually over months
3. **Personalization Increases Over Time:** Your practice will likely become more intuitive and less structured
4. **Different Life Phases Require Adjustments:** Be prepared to modify your approach during major life changes
5. **The Journey Continues Beyond Weight Changes:** Long-term benefits extend far beyond initial physical transformations

Remember that the true success of these first 30 days lies not just in the changes you've experienced but in establishing a foundation for sustainable practice that continues to serve your wellbeing for months and years to come.

The skills you've developed—hunger awareness, flexible consistency, body atonement, challenge navigation—represent valuable tools that will serve you far beyond fasting itself. Whether you continue your current practice, evolve it significantly, or find yourself returning after pauses, the body wisdom you've developed remains accessible.

Your 30-day journey represents not an endpoint but

a beginning—an introduction to a practice that can evolve with you through different seasons of life, continuously adapting to serve your changing needs while maintaining its core benefits. The structured framework has served its purpose in establishing your foundation; now your personal experience becomes your most valuable guide.

CHAPTER 11: BEYOND THE BASICS: QUESTIONS, ANSWERS, AND MOVING FORWARD

The Natural Evolution of Questions

As you progress beyond your initial fasting experience, you'll likely find your questions evolving from basic "how-to" concerns to more nuanced inquiries about sustainability, adaptation, and long-term integration. This evolution reflects your growing experience and the deeper relationship you're developing with your fasting practice.

What makes this chapter different from earlier sections is its focus on the journey beyond the basics—addressing the questions that emerge after you've established your foundation and are looking to refine, sustain, and deepen your practice over time. Rather than presenting these as abstract concepts, I've organized them as conversations addressing the questions most beginners have after their initial adaptation period.

This chapter follows the natural progression of the fasting journey, moving from questions about adapting your practice, through troubleshooting common challenges, into strategies for long-term sustainability, and finally exploring the more advanced dimensions that may interest you as your practice matures.

Start Here If...

This navigational guide helps you locate the specific information most relevant to your current experience:

If you've hit a weight loss plateau: Start with the section on "Adapting When Progress Stalls" to understand plateaus and strategic adjustments.

If you're struggling with consistency: The "Creating Sustainable Motivation" section addresses finding deeper motivation beyond initial enthusiasm.

If social situations remain challenging: See "Navigating Ongoing Social Dynamics" for strategies to handle persistent social pressure or questions.

If your schedule has significantly changed: Begin with "Adapting to Life Transitions" for guidance on modifying your practice during major shifts.

If you're considering extending your fasting windows: Review "Exploring Advanced Approaches" for guidance on safely exploring longer fasts.

If your initial benefits seem to be diminishing: See "Refreshing Your Practice" for strategies to revitalize your approach.

If you're curious about the deeper aspects of fasting: Explore "The Evolving Fasting Journey" to understand how your practice might develop beyond physical benefits.

If you're wondering how research is developing: Check "Emerging Research and Future Directions" for current scientific developments in fasting.

Adapting and Adjusting Your Practice

Q: I've been following the same fasting schedule for several months. Should I change it periodically, or stay consistent?

The question of whether to maintain consistency or introduce strategic variation comes up for many practitioners after their initial success. Both approaches have merit, and your optimal choice depends on several factors:

Benefits of consistency: Maintaining the same fasting schedule simplifies decision-making, establishes stronger habits, and provides clear structure. For many people, this consistency supports long-term adherence and reduces the mental energy required to sustain their practice.

Benefits of periodic variation: Introducing strategic changes can prevent adaptation plateaus, address changing life circumstances, and maintain engagement with your practice. Variation also helps you discover which approaches work best for your unique body under different conditions.

The most sustainable approach for many people is "consistent flexibility"—maintaining a core fasting pattern that remains relatively stable while allowing for intentional variations based on:

1. Body feedback: Adjusting in response to your body's changing signals and needs
2. Life circumstances: Modifying timing around work schedules, social events, or seasonal patterns
3. Experimental curiosity: Periodically testing adjustments to discover optimal approaches
4. Strategic intervention: Introducing changes when progress stalls or benefits plateau

Rather than changing randomly, consider making intentional adjustments while noting how these changes affect your experience. This methodical approach transforms variations from inconsistency into valuable self-experimentation.

Marcus, who has practiced intermittent fasting for over two years, describes his evolution: "I started with strict 16:8 fasting every day because I needed that structure to establish the habit. After about six months, I began introducing strategic variation—extending to 18:6 twice weekly, occasionally practicing one 24-hour fast monthly, and allowing more flexibility on special occasions. These variations keep my practice interesting while the core approach remains consistent."

Q: How do I know if I should extend my fasting window further or stay where I am?

This excellent question reflects the common uncertainty about whether "more is better" when it comes to fasting duration. While longer fasts do intensify certain benefits like autophagy, they aren't necessarily optimal for everyone in all circumstances. Here's how to evaluate whether extending your current window makes sense for you:

Consider extending your fast if:

1. Your current window feels completely comfortable and almost effortless
2. You naturally find yourself extending beyond your planned window without hunger
3. You're curious about additional benefits that longer fasts might provide
4. You've researched and understand the additional considerations for longer fasts
5. Your current health status supports exploring longer periods without food
6. You have appropriate support systems in place for longer fasting periods

Consider maintaining your current window if:

1. Your current practice is delivering the benefits you seek
2. Extending creates significant stress or disruption to your life
3. Your energy, sleep, or mood seem optimal with your current timing
4. You've noticed negative effects when attempting longer fasts previously
5. Your social and family life integrates well with your current schedule
6. Your intuition suggests your current practice feels "right" for your body

The wisest approach is one that honours your body's

feedback above external prescriptions. The "best" fasting window isn't the longest one you can endure, but the one that provides optimal benefits while remaining sustainable and life-enhancing.

Regularly check in with these questions: Am I feeling energized and clear with my current practice? Are the benefits I value continuing? Does my current approach integrate well with my life? If you can answer yes to these questions, there may be no need to extend further, regardless of what others might be practicing.

Q: I've lost weight with intermittent fasting, but I'm concerned about maintaining it long-term. How do I prevent regaining?

This question touches on a legitimate concern, as many weight management approaches show poor long-term sustainability. Intermittent fasting offers several advantages for maintenance, but requires thoughtful transition from initial practice to sustainable long-term approach.

First, understand that weight maintenance differs from weight loss in several important ways:

1. It often allows more flexibility in fasting windows
2. Caloric intake typically increases somewhat from loss phase
3. The focus shifts from changing patterns to sustaining patterns
4. Psychological factors often become more important than physiological ones

Research on successful long-term weight maintenance reveals several key strategies that apply particularly well to intermittent fasting:

1. Maintain core patterns while allowing strategic flexibility: Continue your basic fasting framework while permitting occasional adaptations for life events. This balance prevents the rigid adherence/complete abandonment cycle common in traditional dieting.
2. Focus on identity-based motivation: Shift from outcome-oriented thinking ("I'm fasting to lose weight") to identity-based motivation ("I'm someone who practices intermittent fasting because it makes me feel good"). This subtle but powerful shift supports long-term consistency.
3. Continue regular monitoring: Maintain awareness through some form of tracking —whether formal (periodic weight checks, fasting app, journal) or informal (attention to energy, hunger patterns, clothing fit). This prevents small changes from accumulating unnoticed.
4. Develop sustainable nutritional patterns: While fasting focuses on when you eat, successful maintenance also requires attention to what you eat during eating windows. Focus on nutritional approaches you genuinely enjoy and can maintain indefinitely.
5. Build robust support systems: Connect with communities, individuals, or resources that

normalize and support your continued practice even when initial enthusiasm has faded.
6. Plan for challenging periods: Develop specific strategies for high-risk times like holidays, travel, or stress periods when old patterns might reemerge.
7. Reconnect with non-scale benefits: Regularly remind yourself of the improvements beyond weight that motivate your continued practice—energy, mental clarity, simplified eating patterns, or health markers.

Remember that some physiological adaptation is normal and appropriate as your body establishes its new equilibrium. Small fluctuations within a maintenance range reflect natural body patterns rather than "failure" of your approach.

Q: How do I adapt my fasting practice as I get older?

Our bodies' needs and responses change throughout our lifespan, making periodic reassessment and adaptation of fasting practices both natural and beneficial. While individual variation is significant, certain patterns typically emerge as we age:

Metabolic changes: Many experience slightly decreased metabolic rate and changes in glucose and insulin responses with age. This might mean:

1. Greater benefit from consistent fasting schedules that support metabolic health
2. Potentially higher importance of protein intake during eating windows

3. More attention to overall nutrition quality within compressed eating periods

Hormonal transitions: Major hormonal shifts (like perimenopause and menopause for women or andropause for men) can affect optimal fasting approaches:

1. Some find shorter, more consistent fasting periods work better during these transitions
2. Others benefit from adjusting fasting windows to address specific symptoms like sleep disruption or energy fluctuations
3. Coordination with healthcare providers becomes increasingly important during these transitions

Medication considerations: As medication needs sometimes increase with age, timing considerations become more important:

1. Some medications require food for proper absorption
2. Medication timing might necessitate adjustments to fasting windows
3. Regular medical consultation ensures fasting practice supports overall health management

Muscle preservation focus: Maintaining muscle mass becomes increasingly important with age:

1. Adequate protein intake during eating windows takes on greater significance
2. Resistance training combined with appropriate fasting windows supports muscle health

3. Some older adults benefit from slightly shorter fasting periods with higher protein density during eating windows

Rather than viewing these adaptations as limitations, consider them refinements that honour your body's changing needs. Fasting practice can evolve throughout your lifespan, continuing to provide benefits when appropriately adjusted to your current physiology.

Margaret, who began intermittent fasting at 49 and has continued through her transition into menopause at 52, shares her experience: "I've had to become more flexible with my approach as my body has changed. During perimenopause, I found shorter fasts of 12-14 hours worked better, paired with more attention to protein intake. Now post-menopause, I've been able to return to 16-hour fasts most days, but I'm much more attentive to how my body responds and adjust accordingly. The practice has helped me navigate this transition with better energy and fewer symptoms than many friends who don't fast."

Troubleshooting Common Challenges

Q: I've hit a plateau where I'm no longer seeing the benefits I initially experienced. What should I do?

Plateaus are natural parts of any health practice, including intermittent fasting. Rather than indicators of failure, they represent opportunities for refinement and deeper understanding. Several approaches can help you move beyond current plateaus:

1. Assess whether it's truly a plateau: Sometimes

benefits continue accruing in areas you're not monitoring. Before making changes, expand your awareness beyond your initial focus (often weight) to notice changes in energy, sleep quality, mental clarity, or mood. You may discover ongoing improvements in areas you hadn't been tracking.

2. Introduce strategic variation: After consistent practice, your body adapts to your fasting pattern—a sign of successful metabolic flexibility. Introducing periodic variation can stimulate further adaptation:
    a. Occasionally extend or shorten your fasting window
    b. Try one longer fast (24 hours) once weekly or monthly if appropriate for your health status
    c. Experiment with different fasting window timing (morning vs. evening fasting)
    d. Consider alternating different fasting approaches throughout the week

3. Review eating window quality: Sometimes plateaus reflect nutritional patterns during eating windows rather than fasting issues:
    a. Assess whether calorie intake has unconsciously increased as your body adapted
    b. Review macronutrient balance, particularly protein adequacy
    c. Consider whether processed food consumption has gradually increased

d. Evaluate portions and mindfulness during eating windows

4. Address lifestyle factors beyond fasting:
   a. Sleep quality and duration significantly affect metabolic response
   b. Stress management impacts hormonal balance and fat storage
   c. Movement patterns influence metabolic health alongside fasting
   d. Alcohol consumption can affect fasting benefits, particularly liver function

5. Deepen your practice qualitatively:
   a. Increase mindfulness during both fasting and eating periods
   b. Develop greater body awareness of hunger, energy, and satiety signals
   c. Explore the emotional and psychological dimensions of your relationship with food
   d. Connect your practice to broader health and life values beyond initial goals

Remember that some plateaus represent your body finding its natural equilibrium rather than problems to be solved. The goal isn't perpetual linear improvement but rather sustainable health and wellbeing that you can maintain long-term.

Q: I was consistent with fasting for months but got completely off track after vacation. How do I restart effectively?

This experience is incredibly common and represents a natural part of developing any sustainable health practice. Rather than viewing your break as failure, recognize it as an opportunity to develop "restart resilience"—the ability to return to beneficial practices after interruptions.

The most effective restart approach typically includes:

1. Begin with self-compassion: Acknowledge that perfect consistency isn't required for benefits and that learning to restart is actually a valuable skill. This compassionate mindset prevents the common "failure spiral" where temporary interruptions become permanent abandonment.

2. Start more gradually than your previous practice: Rather than immediately attempting to resume your most advanced practice, begin with a gentler approach—perhaps 12-14 hour fasts instead of 16-18 hours. This gradual re-entry reduces both physical and psychological resistance.

3. Focus on completion rather than perfection: Set easily achievable goals for your first week back—perhaps just three successful fasting days regardless of duration. These "wins" rebuild momentum and confidence in your capacity.

4. Review what worked before: Reflect on the specific strategies, times, and approaches that

supported your previous successful practice. Reimplement these proven methods rather than starting from scratch.

5. Identify what derailed your practice: Was it the schedule disruption? Social pressure? Changed environment? Understanding the specific challenges helps you develop targeted strategies for similar situations in the future.

6. Create stronger environmental supports: After a break, external structures become particularly important. Consider using:
    a. Fasting apps with reminders
    b. Accountability partners
    c. Visual cues in your environment
    d. Pre-planned meals for eating windows
    e. Morning routines that support fasting intention

7. Connect with your deeper motivation: Beyond physical outcomes, reconnect with how fasting makes you feel—increased energy, mental clarity, simplified relationship with food, or other personal benefits that matter to you.

Restart experiences are valuable learning opportunities that ultimately strengthen your practice by developing flexibility and resilience. Many long-term practitioners report that learning to restart effectively was actually more valuable than uninterrupted consistency because life inevitably includes periods of disruption.

Q: I'm finding it increasingly difficult to stick with my

fasting schedule. Is this normal or a sign I should stop?

This common experience can stem from several different sources, each suggesting a different response. Let's explore the possibilities:

If your waning motivation stems from boredom or routine fatigue: This normal response to any repeated practice can be addressed through mindful variation—adjusting your fasting window timing, trying different fasting-friendly beverages, creating new morning rituals, or periodically experimenting with different fasting approaches. These refreshing changes maintain the core benefits while preventing monotony.

If difficulty arises from changing life circumstances: Your optimal fasting approach naturally evolves with your changing life—new work schedules, family responsibilities, or living situations. Rather than abandoning your practice, adapt it to your current reality. Sometimes a temporary shift to shorter fasting windows or fewer fasting days maintains the foundation while accommodating new demands.

If physical discomfort has increased: Return to basics—review your hydration, electrolyte balance, and eating window nutrition. Sometimes gradually developed habits like decreased water intake or reduced protein consumption create physical challenges that can be easily addressed. If discomfort persists despite adjustments, consult healthcare providers to ensure your current approach remains appropriate for your health status.

If you've lost connection with your purpose: Initial

motivation often comes from external goals like weight loss, while sustainable motivation emerges from deeper values and experienced benefits. Reconnect with how fasting enhances your daily experience—energy, clarity, freedom from constant food concerns, or other personal benefits. Journaling about these benefits can reawaken your intrinsic motivation.

If your social environment has become challenging: Sustained resistance from family, friends, or colleagues can gradually erode your commitment. Consider whether you need to have more direct conversations about your needs, find additional support communities, or develop clearer boundaries around food discussions.

The key distinction is whether your challenge represents a need for adjustment or a genuine signal to discontinue. For most people, waning motivation indicates a need for practice refinement rather than abandonment. However, if your difficulty persists despite thoughtful adjustments, or if physical symptoms concern you, consulting healthcare providers ensures you're making informed decisions about continuing or modifying your practice.

Long-term Sustainability Strategies

Q: How do I create sustainable motivation after the initial excitement fades?

This question touches on a critical transition in any health practice—moving from the motivation of novelty and rapid initial changes to a sustainable source of commitment that withstands the test of time.

Research on long-term behaviour maintenance reveals several powerful strategies:

1. Shift from outcome motivation to process motivation: Initially, many are motivated by anticipated results like weight loss or improved health markers. Sustainable motivation often comes from enjoying the actual practice itself—appreciating the mental clarity during fasting periods, valuing the simplicity of fewer meal decisions, or welcoming the relationship with hunger as interesting rather than threatening.
2. Connect to identity and values: Frame your practice in terms of who you want to be rather than what you want to achieve. "I'm someone who values mental clarity and energy, which intermittent fasting helps me maintain" creates stronger motivation than "I'm trying to lose weight through fasting." This identity-based motivation persists even when visible progress plateaus.
3. Develop meaningful rituals: Create enjoyable routines that support your fasting practice—perhaps a special morning tea during fasting periods, a mindful meal to break your fast, or a brief reflection practice during fasting windows. These rituals transform fasting from deprivation to meaningful practice.
4. Find the right accountability balance: External accountability helps many maintain consistency, but the form matters significantly. Look for supportive

accountability that celebrates consistency rather than punishes deviation. This might come through apps, communities, partners, or personal tracking methods that work with your temperament.
5. Practice self-compassionate consistency: Perfectionistic approaches typically fail long-term, while rigid rules often provoke rebellion. Instead, aim for "flexible consistency"—a practice reliable enough to deliver benefits while adaptable enough to accommodate life's realities.
6. Periodically refresh your awareness: Long-term practices often become background habits where benefits fade from conscious awareness. Periodically check in with how different you feel during temporary departures from your practice (like vacations or holidays). These contrasts often reawaken appreciation for your regular fasting benefits.
7. Connect with community: Sharing experiences with others who practice intermittent fasting normalizes your approach and provides fresh motivation through others' insights and successes. These connections prevent the isolation that can undermine long-term commitment.

Remember that motivation naturally fluctuates. The goal isn't maintaining constant high enthusiasm but rather developing multiple motivation sources that collectively sustain your practice through inevitable ebbs and flows of interest and energy.

Q: How should I adjust my fasting practice during major life transitions like changing jobs or moving?

Major life transitions present both challenges and opportunities for your fasting practice. With thoughtful navigation, these periods can actually strengthen your approach by developing adaptability and demonstrating how fasting can support you through change. Consider these strategies:

1. Temporarily simplify your approach: During major transitions, cognitive and emotional resources are often strained. Simplifying your fasting practice—perhaps using a slightly shorter but very consistent window—reduces the decision-making burden while maintaining core benefits.
2. Prioritize consistency over duration: Maintaining a consistent daily rhythm, even with modified timing, provides valuable structure during otherwise unsettled periods. This consistency can serve as a grounding practice amid change.
3. Plan transition strategies in advance: Before the change begins, develop specific plans for how you'll maintain your practice during different phases of the transition. Having predetermined strategies reduces in-the-moment decisions when willpower may be depleted.
4. Focus on the stabilizing benefits: During transitions, fasting's cognitive and emotional benefits often prove particularly valuable—

mental clarity for decision-making, energy for managing change, and emotional regulation during stress. Recognizing these benefits strengthens motivation to maintain your practice.
5. Create environmental triggers in your new setting: When physical environments change, established habits often need reinforcement. Identify specific environmental cues in your new setting that will support your fasting rhythm—perhaps a special water bottle on your new desk, a particular tea mug that signals fasting periods, or alarms on your phone that transcend location changes.
6. Build flexibility with core minimums: Establish the minimum practice you'll maintain during the most demanding transition periods. Perhaps this means 12-hour fasts five days weekly instead of your usual 16-hour daily fasts. This minimum maintains the foundation of your practice while accommodating temporary disruption.
7. Use fasting as a transitional tool rather than an additional stressor: Frame your practice as supporting your wellbeing during change rather than an additional obligation. This perspective shift helps prevent fasting from becoming another source of pressure during already challenging times.

Remember that successfully adapting your practice through major life changes builds valuable resilience and flexibility. Many long-term practitioners report that navigating transitions actually strengthened their relationship with fasting by demonstrating its adaptability to different life circumstances.

Q: How do I handle ongoing social pressure or questions about my eating schedule?

Navigating the social dimensions of intermittent fasting often requires more sophisticated strategies as time passes. While initial questions might be satisfied with simple explanations, persistent social pressure or recurring questions benefit from more developed approaches:

1. Develop tiered responses based on relationship depth: Create several explanation levels—from brief responses for casual inquiries to more detailed explanations for those genuinely interested:
    a. Casual response: "I've found this eating pattern gives me better energy throughout the day."
    b. Moderate explanation: "I practice time-restricted eating, which helps my energy and focus. It works well with my schedule."
    c. Detailed discussion (for genuinely interested people): An honest conversation about your experience, benefits, and approach.
2. Shift from defensiveness to ownership: Rather than feeling you need to justify your choices, practice confident ownership of your approach. The difference between "I can't eat now because I'm fasting" and "I prefer eating

later in the day" is subtle but significant in how others perceive and respect your choices.
3. Recognize concern versus criticism: Sometimes questions stem from genuine concern rather than criticism. Acknowledging the care behind questions often changes the interaction's tone: "I appreciate your concern about me skipping breakfast. I've found this approach really works for my body, and I'm monitoring how it affects me."
4. Set clear boundaries when needed: For persistent questioning or pressure, more direct boundary-setting may be appropriate: "I understand you have different views on eating patterns, but I've found this approach works well for me. I'd prefer we focus our conversations on other topics when we're together."
5. Find social eating compromises: For regular social gatherings centred around meals outside your eating window, consider:
    a. Occasionally adjusting your eating window for special events
    b. Suggesting alternative activities that don't centre around food
    c. Participating without eating, focusing on the social connection
    d. Proposing different timing that aligns better with your eating window
6. Connect with like-minded community: Building relationships with others who practice intermittent fasting provides social spaces where your eating pattern is

normalized rather than questioned. These connections often provide valuable emotional support.
7. Remember that your health practices are personal choices: While considerate explanation often helps relationships, you don't ultimately need others' approval for your health decisions. Confidence in your approach, based on your personal experience and research, provides foundation when facing persistent questioning.

Most social resistance diminishes over time as others observe your consistent practice and wellbeing. What initially generates questions often eventually earns respect as your sustained commitment and benefits become apparent.

Special Situations and Circumstances

Q: How should I adapt fasting during periods of high stress or when I'm not sleeping well?

The relationship between fasting, stress, and sleep deserves special attention because these elements significantly influence each other. During periods of elevated stress or poor sleep, thoughtful fasting adaptations can support resilience rather than adding additional strain to your system.

First, understand the physiological connections:

1. Stress increases cortisol, which affects both hunger and fat storage patterns
2. Sleep deprivation alters hunger hormones,

typically increasing appetite
3. Both stress and poor sleep can temporarily decrease insulin sensitivity
4. Fasting itself represents a mild hormetic stressor on your body

Given these connections, consider these adaptive approaches:

1. Shorter but consistent fasting periods: During high stress or poor sleep, maintaining shorter fasting periods (12-14 hours rather than 16-18) often provides metabolic benefits without adding excessive stress to your system. This moderation honours your current circumstances while maintaining basic practice.

2. Focus on fasting quality rather than duration: When stress is high, emphasize proper hydration, electrolyte balance, and complete nutrition during eating windows rather than pushing fasting length. These elements support your body's stress response capacity.

3. Prioritize sleep-supporting practices: During periods of sleep disruption, adjust your eating window to best support sleep quality:
    a. Consider earlier eating windows that close at least 2-3 hours before bedtime
    b. Include foods containing natural melatonin precursors in your evening meal
    c. Moderate or eliminate alcohol, which disrupts sleep architecture despite its

relaxing effects

4. Add stress-reduction practices during fasting periods: Transform fasting windows into opportunities for stress management by incorporating:
    a. Brief meditation sessions during typical eating times
    b. Gentle movement like walking or stretching when hunger appears
    c. Nature exposure during morning fasting hours
    d. Breathwork techniques when feeling stressed during fasts

5. Consider stress timing in relation to fasting windows: Some people find fasting during their most stressful hours challenging, while others experience greater clarity and resilience during fasted states. Notice your personal pattern and adjust accordingly—perhaps fasting during lower-stress periods and eating during peak stress if that serves your wellbeing.

6. Use flexible consistency: Rather than abandoning your practice entirely during stressful periods, find the modified version you can maintain consistently. This approach preserves the foundation of your practice while honouring your current needs.

Remember that temporary adjustments during high-stress periods represent wisdom rather than weakness. The most sustainable long-term practice includes thoughtful adaptation to your changing life circumstances rather than rigid adherence regardless of context.

Q: How do I adapt my fasting schedule when traveling across time zones?

Travel across time zones presents unique challenges for intermittent fasting but also opportunities to use fasting strategically for better travel experiences. With thoughtful planning, your fasting practice can actually help reduce jet lag while maintaining consistency despite changing environments.

Consider these strategies for different travel scenarios:

For travel days themselves:

1. Use fasting strategically during travel to reduce jet lag by fasting during the flight and breaking your fast at an appropriate meal time at your destination. Research suggests this helps reset your circadian rhythm more quickly.
2. Focus on hydration during travel, as dehydration exacerbates both jet lag and fasting discomfort. Bring an empty water bottle through security and fill it before boarding, or request regular water refills from flight attendants.
3. Plan your eating window based on destination time rather than departure time when crossing multiple zones. This forward-focusing helps your body begin adapting to the new schedule.

4. Consider a modified fasting approach like 12:12 during the first day of significant time zone changes, providing structure without additional stress during adaptation.

For short trips (2-4 days):
1. Decide whether adapting to the new time zone makes sense for very short trips. Sometimes maintaining your home eating schedule (adjusted for clock time) works better for brief travel.
2. If adapting to local time, use fasting to facilitate faster adjustment by immediately implementing eating windows based on destination timing.
3. Focus on maintaining consistency in fasting duration even if timing shifts to accommodate local schedules.

For longer trips:
1. Adapt your eating window to local time, typically following the same fasting duration but adjusted to appropriate local meal times.
2. Be patient with your body's adaptation, which typically takes 1-2 days per time zone crossed for complete adjustment.
3. Use environmental cues like morning sunlight exposure to help reset your circadian rhythm alongside your fasting schedule.
4. Create simple systems for maintaining awareness of fasting times in new environments, such as setting alarms on your phone or creating calendar reminders.

For all travel scenarios:
1. Pack fasting-friendly items like electrolyte supplements, herbal tea bags, and a reusable water bottle to maintain your fasting support tools while traveling.
2. Plan in advance how you'll handle social meals or business dinners that might conflict with your preferred fasting schedule.
3. Consider relaxing rigid fasting rules when travel involves unique cultural food experiences that represent significant value beyond nutrition.
4. Remember that maintaining some fasting structure, even if modified, provides valuable consistency during the disruptions of travel.

The key principle is using fasting as a tool to enhance your travel experience rather than a rigid practice that creates additional stress. With this balanced approach, many travellers find their fasting practice actually improves their adaptation to new time zones while providing helpful structure amid changing environments.

Q: Should I adjust my fasting approach during illness or recovery?

Navigating fasting during illness or recovery periods requires particular attention to your body's specific needs. While some fasting approaches may support certain aspects of recovery, others might hinder healing processes that require additional resources. Here's guidance for different scenarios:

During acute illness (colds, flu, infections):

1. Consider temporarily shortening or pausing fasting, particularly during high fever, active infection, or significant symptoms. Your body often needs additional nutritional resources and regular energy availability to mount effective immune responses.
2. Focus on nutrient density during eating windows if continuing modified fasting. Ensure adequate protein, vitamins, minerals, and hydration to support immune function and recovery.
3. Listen to appetite cues, which often provide valuable information during illness. Lack of hunger during mild illness may indicate your body benefiting from decreased food intake, while strong hunger might signal need for additional resources.
4. Consult healthcare providers for illnesses requiring medical attention, especially regarding how fasting might interact with medications or treatment protocols.

During recovery from injury or surgery:

1. Prioritize protein intake and nutrient timing to support tissue repair, which often requires more frequent nutrient availability than standard fasting protocols allow.
2. Consider shorter fasting periods (12-14 hours rather than 16+) to ensure adequate nutritional resources for healing while maintaining some metabolic benefits of

fasting.

3. Coordinate with healthcare providers about optimal nutrition timing, particularly following procedures with specific nutritional recommendations.
4. Remember that healing represents additional metabolic demand beyond your normal requirements. Fasting approaches appropriate during health might be insufficient during recovery periods.

During chronic condition management:

1. Work closely with knowledgeable healthcare providers to determine how fasting might complement or potentially complicate your specific condition management.
2. Consider how your medications interact with fasting states—some medications require food for proper absorption or function, while others may work differently during fasted states.
3. Monitor your symptoms and recovery markers closely when implementing fasting alongside chronic condition management, adjusting as needed based on your body's responses.
4. Balance potential benefits against risks, recognizing that more moderate fasting approaches often provide benefits with fewer potential complications during chronic health management.

The wisdom principle during illness or recovery is prioritizing your body's healing resources over fasting ideals. Temporarily modifying or pausing your fasting practice during acute illness or recovery represents self-care rather than inconsistency. Many practitioners find their return to fasting after appropriate recovery periods actually results in enhanced benefits compared to pushing through illness with unmodified fasting.

Advanced Fasting Considerations

Q: I'm interested in trying longer fasts (24+ hours). What should I know before attempting them?

Extending your fasting practice beyond the typical 16-18 hour windows represents a significant step that requires additional preparation, knowledge, and support. While longer fasts can offer enhanced benefits for some individuals, they also involve distinct considerations:

Potential Benefits of Extended Fasting:

1. Deeper autophagy (cellular cleaning processes)
2. More pronounced ketosis and metabolic switching
3. Potentially stronger inflammatory reduction
4. Extended periods of mental clarity for some practitioners
5. Deeper relationship with hunger and satisfaction cycles

Important Preparatory Steps:

1. Ensure medical appropriateness:
    a. Consult healthcare providers, particularly if you have any existing health conditions
    b. Consider baseline testing of relevant

health markers before beginning
   c. Identify any specific contraindications for your unique health situation

2. Build a strong foundation:
   a. Establish consistent comfort with 16-20 hour fasts before attempting 24+ hours
   b. Develop solid understanding of electrolyte needs and hydration strategies
   c. Create reliable hunger management techniques from your existing practice

3. Educate yourself specifically about longer fasts:
   a. Understand the typical progression of sensations beyond your familiar fasting duration
   b. Learn appropriate breaking-fast protocols for longer fasts
   c. Research how medication timing might need adjustment for extended fasting periods

4. Create supportive conditions:
   a. Select appropriate timing when stress is lower and schedule demands are manageable
   b. Ensure adequate sleep before beginning longer fasts
   c. Plan activities that complement rather than complicate the experience

Implementation Recommendations:

1. Start modestly:
    a. Begin with a single 24-hour fast rather than multi-day fasting
    b. Choose a convenient period, often from dinner to dinner the following day
    c. Ensure you can rest if needed during your first extended fast
2. Prioritize proper hydration and electrolytes:
    a. Increase water intake during extended fasts
    b. Incorporate appropriate electrolytes (sodium, potassium, magnesium)
    c. Monitor for signs of electrolyte imbalance like headaches, dizziness, or heart palpitations
3. Plan your fast-breaking meal carefully:
    a. Research appropriate foods for breaking longer fasts
    b. Begin with easily digestible smaller portions rather than large meals
    c. Allow time for digestive readjustment before consuming difficult-to-digest foods
4. Monitor your response thoroughly:
    a. Keep notes on physical, emotional, and cognitive experiences
    b. Track energy, mood, sleep quality, and recovery afterward
    c. Use this information to determine whether and how to incorporate longer fasts in your practice

Safety Considerations:

1. Recognize signs that indicate breaking your fast early might be appropriate
2. Have support people aware of your fasting practice in case you need assistance
3. Be particularly cautious if taking medications or managing health conditions
4. Differentiate between normal fasting discomfort and potential warning signs

Extended fasting represents an advanced practice that isn't necessary or appropriate for everyone. Many people receive significant benefits from standard intermittent fasting approaches without venturing into longer durations. The decision to explore extended fasting should emerge from genuine curiosity and appropriate preparation rather than assumptions that longer necessarily means better.

Q: How do I know if I'm ready to try more advanced fasting approaches?

Assessing your readiness for advanced fasting approaches involves honestly evaluating several dimensions of your current practice and overall wellbeing. This self-assessment helps ensure you're building upon a solid foundation rather than prematurely advancing to more challenging protocols.

Consider these readiness indicators:

Physiological Readiness:

1. You consistently complete your current fasting

protocol with relative ease
2. Your energy remains stable throughout your fasting periods
3. You've resolved initial adaptation challenges like headaches or excessive hunger
4. Your sleep quality remains good with your current fasting approach
5. You recover well after your current fasting periods without excessive fatigue
6. Your body weight has stabilized at a healthy level for your frame

Psychological Readiness:

1. You approach fasting with curiosity rather than rigid perfectionism
2. You can distinguish between habitual eating urges and genuine body needs
3. You've developed effective strategies for managing discomfort during fasting
4. You maintain emotional balance during fasting periods
5. You can adjust your approach without self-judgment when circumstances require
6. Your relationship with food during eating windows feels balanced rather than restrictive or excessive

Knowledge Foundation:

1. You understand the physiological processes that occur during different fasting durations
2. You're familiar with appropriate hydration and electrolyte needs for longer fasts

3. You've researched proper techniques for breaking extended fasts
4. You've considered how longer fasts might interact with your specific health conditions or medications
5. You're aware of warning signs that would indicate when to end a fast early

Support Structure:

1. You have appropriate medical guidance if managing health conditions
2. You've developed support systems that understand and respect your practice
3. You have reliable resources for answering questions that might arise
4. You've created environmental conditions that support successful fasting

Motivational Clarity:

1. You have clear, well-considered reasons for exploring advanced approaches
2. Your motivation extends beyond weight loss to broader health understanding
3. You approach advancement with patience rather than urgency
4. You're prepared to learn from the experience regardless of outcome

If most of these indicators align with your current experience, you may be ready to thoughtfully explore more advanced approaches. If significant gaps remain, focusing on strengthening your foundation before advancing will likely create more sustainable long-term success.

Remember that fasting depth isn't a competition, and many practitioners find their optimal benefits from consistent moderate approaches rather than more extreme protocols. The "best" practice is ultimately the one that enhances your overall wellbeing while integrating sustainably into your life.

Try This Now: Future Vision Exercise

This visualization exercise helps connect your current practice with your longer-term fasting journey, strengthening motivation and clarifying your personal path:

1. Find a comfortable seated position in a quiet space. Close your eyes and take five deep, relaxing breaths.
2. Imagine yourself one year from now, having maintained and refined your fasting practice. Visualize yourself in detail—how you move, how you feel in your body, your energy level, your relationship with hunger and food.
3. See yourself navigating a typical day with your evolved fasting practice. Notice:
    a. How naturally your fasting windows flow within your day
    b. The ease with which you transition between fasted and fed states
    c. How you approach meals with presence and enjoyment
    d. The clarity and focus you bring to your activities
4. Visualize yourself successfully handling

situations that currently challenge your practice:
   a. Navigating social meals with confidence
   b. Adapting your approach during travel or special occasions
   c. Listening to your body's changing needs with wisdom
   d. Explaining your practice to others when appropriate
5. Connect with the benefits you're experiencing in this future vision:
   a. How does your body feel? Notice energy, comfort, and vitality
   b. How has your mental state evolved? Notice clarity, focus, and emotional balance
   c. How has your relationship with food transformed? Notice freedom, enjoyment, and ease
   d. What broader life aspects have improved through your practice? Notice relationships, work, creativity, or other dimensions
6. Now visualize yourself five years into your practice. How has your approach matured? What wisdom have you developed? How has fasting become integrated into your identity and lifestyle in sustainable ways?
7. Slowly return your awareness to the present moment, bringing with you the feeling of possibility and direction from this vision.
8. Take a few moments to jot down insights

or aspects of this vision that felt particularly meaningful or motivating.

This visualization isn't about creating rigid expectations but rather developing an evolving vision that guides your journey. You might revisit and revise this vision periodically as your experience and understanding deepen.

The Evolving Fasting Journey

Q: How does fasting practice typically change as practitioners gain experience?

The evolution of fasting practice tends to follow fascinating patterns as practitioners move from beginners to experienced fasters. Understanding these typical developmental stages can help normalize your experience and provide perspective on your personal journey.

Most practitioners evolve through several phases, though the timing and specific manifestations vary individually:

Initial Phase: Protocol Focus In early stages, most practitioners concentrate primarily on "doing it right"—following specific timeframes, permitted beverages, and technical rules. This foundation-building stage typically involves:

1. Close tracking of fasting hours
2. Concern with whether specific items break a fast
3. Achievement orientation around completing target windows

4. External validation and guidance seeking

This protocol focus serves an important purpose in establishing basic patterns and understanding. However, most practitioners naturally evolve beyond this mechanical approach as their experience deepens.

Intermediate Phase: Pattern Recognition With continued practice, awareness typically shifts from external rules to noticing personal patterns and responses:

- Recognizing your unique hunger cycles
1. Observing energy fluctuations throughout fasting and eating periods
2. Connecting mood and mental clarity to specific fasting durations
3. Noticing how different foods affect subsequent fasting ease
4. Developing personal preferences for fasting window timing

This pattern recognition phase significantly enhances your ability to personalize your approach based on direct experience rather than generic recommendations.

Advanced Phase: Principle Integration Experienced practitioners often move beyond rigid schedules to a principle-based approach:

1. Understanding the underlying mechanisms well enough to adapt flexibly
2. Developing intuitive awareness of when to extend or shorten fasting periods

3. Making adjustments based on body feedback and life circumstances
4. Balancing consistency with appropriate flexibility
5. Focusing on quality of fasting experience rather than just duration

This integration phase typically creates greater sustainability as fasting becomes more aligned with your unique needs and circumstances.

Mature Phase: Intuitive Practice The most experienced practitioners often develop what might be called "intuitive fasting":

1. Fasting windows that flow naturally with minimal tracking or monitoring
2. Deepened body awareness that guides eating timing
3. Flexible adaptation to changing life circumstances
4. Integration of fasting with broader health and life philosophy
5. Focus on qualitative experience rather than quantitative measures

This mature phase represents fasting as a fully integrated life practice rather than a separate health intervention requiring constant attention.

Understanding this evolution helps normalize the changes in your relationship with fasting over time. The initial protocol focus isn't meant to remain rigid indefinitely; the natural progression toward more intuitive practice represents growth rather than inconsistency.

Q: How can I tell if my fasting practice is actually benefiting me long-term?

This thoughtful question reflects the wisdom of periodically evaluating whether your practice continues serving your overall wellbeing rather than becoming an end in itself. Several approaches can help you assess the genuine value of your continued practice:

1. Conduct periodic comprehensive assessments beyond single measurements:
    a. Physical indicators: Energy levels, sleep quality, digestive comfort, physical resilience
    b. Mental aspects: Cognitive clarity, focus duration, memory function, creative capacity
    c. Emotional dimensions: Mood stability, stress response, emotional regulation
    d. Relationship factors: Food freedom, social ease around eating, balanced approach
2. Evaluate sustainability markers that indicate healthy integration:
    a. Does your practice flex appropriately with life circumstances?
    b. Can you maintain your approach without excessive mental preoccupation?
    c. Does fasting enhance rather than compete with other life dimensions?

d. Do you approach your practice with curiosity and flexibility rather than rigid rules?

3. Consider contrast experiences that provide comparative information:
   a. How do you feel during periods when your practice is interrupted (vacations, illness)?
   b. Do you notice meaningful differences when returning to your practice after breaks?
   c. Has your baseline wellbeing improved compared to your pre-fasting state?
   d. Do objective health markers show positive trends with your continued practice?

4. Reflect on your relationship with the practice itself:
   a. Does fasting feel like a supportive tool or an obligatory burden?
   b. Has your motivation evolved from external outcomes to intrinsic benefits?
   c. Do you approach hunger and eating with greater awareness and choice?
   d. Has your relationship with food during eating windows improved?

5. Seek balanced external input from trusted sources:
   a. Feedback from healthcare providers on relevant health markers

b. Observations from close friends or family about your overall wellbeing
  c. Input from experienced fasting practitioners about your approach
  d. Current research on long-term effects of your specific fasting pattern

The most telling indicator often comes from honestly answering this question: If all external validation and expectations were removed, would you continue this practice based solely on how it makes you feel and function? The answer reveals whether your practice has become authentically valuable to you beyond social reinforcement or identity attachment.

Remember that beneficial practices can still benefit from periodic adjustments. Even if your assessment confirms fasting's value, remaining open to refinements based on your evolving life circumstances and deepening body awareness ensures your practice continues serving your highest wellbeing.

Emerging Research and Future Directions

Q: How is scientific understanding of fasting continuing to evolve?

The research landscape around intermittent fasting continues to develop rapidly, with several exciting directions emerging in recent years. While maintaining appropriate scientific caution about preliminary findings, these research areas suggest interesting possibilities for future fasting applications and optimizations:

Chrononutrition and Timing Specificity Recent

research increasingly suggests that when we eat may be as important as what we eat, with particular attention to aligning eating windows with natural circadian rhythms:

1. Studies examining whether morning-focused eating windows produce different metabolic effects than evening-focused windows
2. Research on how individual chronotypes (morning vs. evening preference) might affect optimal fasting timing
3. Investigation into how eating window timing affects specific body systems like liver function, heart health, and brain health

Fasting and Microbiome Health Emerging research explores how fasting periods affect our gut microbiome:

1. Studies on how fasting duration impacts microbial diversity
2. Research examining whether fasting creates distinctive microbial rhythms
3. Investigation into connections between fasting-induced microbiome changes and broader health outcomes
4. Exploration of how specific foods during eating windows might complement fasting effects on gut health

Fasting Mimicking Approaches Research continues exploring whether certain nutritional patterns might provide similar benefits to complete fasting while reducing difficulty:

1. Evidence on whether protein restriction alone might activate certain fasting pathways
2. Studies on specific nutritional combinations that may maintain some fasting benefits while allowing some food intake
3. Research on whether particular supplements might enhance fasting benefits without breaking fasts

Personalized Fasting Protocols An exciting frontier involves understanding how individual differences affect optimal fasting approaches:

1. Genetic factors that might influence ideal fasting duration or timing
2. Metabolic testing to identify personalized fasting windows
3. Research on how age, sex, health status, and fitness level interact with different fasting protocols
4. Investigation into whether fasting benefits follow universal or highly individualized patterns

Fasting and Disease-Specific Applications Research continues exploring fasting's potential therapeutic applications:

1. Studies on fasting as complementary support during cancer treatments
2. Research on neurological applications for conditions like Alzheimer's and Parkinson's
3. Investigation into autoimmune condition management with various fasting approaches

4. Exploration of metabolic disorder treatment and prevention through targeted fasting protocols

Psychological Dimensions of Fasting Emerging research examines fasting's effects beyond physical health:

1. Studies on cognitive function during different fasting durations
2. Research on mood regulation and psychological wellbeing with consistent fasting
3. Investigation into potential effects on focus, attention, and executive function
4. Exploration of how fasting might affect stress resilience and emotional regulation

While these research directions offer exciting possibilities, it's important to approach emerging findings with appropriate scientific caution. Single studies often receive disproportionate media attention before replication confirms results. The most reliable approach combines awareness of current research with personal experimentation to determine what works best for your unique body and circumstances.

Q: How do I separate solid information from trends and fads in fasting?

Distinguishing evidence-based information from trending claims presents a significant challenge in the fasting world, where social media can amplify unverified approaches while research evolves rapidly. These evaluation tools help you assess information quality:

1. Source Assessment: Evaluate where the information originates:
    a. Peer-reviewed research in established journals provides stronger evidence than anecdotal reports
    b. Information from researchers actively studying fasting typically offers more reliable insight than general health influencers
    c. Multiple converging sources suggest greater reliability than single-source claims
    d. Authors who acknowledge limitations and uncertainties often demonstrate greater scientific integrity than those making absolute claims

2. Evidence Quality Evaluation: Assess the type and strength of supporting evidence:
    a. Human studies provide more directly applicable evidence than animal research
    b. Larger studies generally offer stronger evidence than smaller ones
    c. Randomized controlled trials provide stronger evidence than observational studies
    d. Studies with longer durations better address sustainability than short-term trials
    e. Replication across multiple studies suggests greater reliability than single-study findings

3. Check for Mechanistic Explanation: Strong claims should include plausible explanations of how the proposed approach works:
    a. Coherent physiological mechanisms based on established science
    b. Explanations that align with broader biological understanding
    c. Recognition of bodily systems' complexity rather than oversimplified mechanisms
    d. Appropriate distinction between hypothesized and confirmed mechanisms

4. Examine Benefit Claims Critically:
    a. Beware of approaches claiming to magnify benefits without trade-offs
    b. Question claims of universal benefit regardless of individual differences
    c. Be sceptical of dramatic results promised in short timeframes
    d. Notice whether potential limitations or contraindications are acknowledged

5. Follow the Money:
    a. Consider whether information sources have financial interests in specific fasting approaches
    b. Be particularly cautious about claims attached to supplement sales or program memberships
    c. Question whether testimonials

represent typical results or carefully selected outliers
d. Notice whether information seems designed primarily to drive purchases or genuinely inform

6. Apply Evolutionary and Historical Context:
   a. Consider whether approaches align with historical human eating patterns
   b. Question modernized approaches that lack historical precedent without clear justification
   c. Be cautious of claims that require multiple modern supplements to implement safely

7. Trust Your Experience Wisely:
   a. Value your direct experience while recognizing its individual nature
   b. Distinguish between immediate sensations and long-term effects
   c. Consider whether perceived benefits might result from factors beyond the specific approach
   d. Remain open to adjusting based on both personal experience and emerging evidence

The hallmark of quality information typically includes nuance, appropriate caution about generalization, recognition of individual variation, and transparent acknowledgment of what remains unknown. Sources that present complex topics with inappropriate certainty or promise universal results regardless of individual factors often indicate lower information quality regardless of their popularity.

A Long-Term Success Story: The Evolution of Practice

Catherine's journey with intermittent fasting spans over five years, providing valuable perspective on how a sustainable practice evolves over time. Her experience illustrates many common patterns in long-term fasting integration while highlighting principles that support genuine sustainability.

When Catherine began intermittent fasting at 38, she was primarily motivated by weight management concerns after struggling with gradual weight gain throughout her 30s. "I started with the popular 16:8 approach because it seemed straightforward," she explains. "Initially, I tracked my fasting hours obsessively, followed all the 'rules' about allowed beverages, and felt like I was either succeeding or failing each day based on whether I completed my full 16 hours."

This protocol-focused beginning—common among most beginners—provided necessary structure during Catherine's adaptation phase. However, as months passed, her practice began evolving in ways that reflect typical long-term development.

"After about six months, I found myself naturally shifting from focusing on exact hours to noticing patterns in my body's responses," Catherine recalls. "I realized that some days, 18 hours felt completely natural, while other days—particularly before my menstrual cycle—14 hours was more appropriate. This awareness helped me develop a more personalized approach based on my body's feedback rather than rigid external standards."

This transition from protocol adherence to body awareness represents a significant developmental milestone that many successful practitioners experience. Rather than abandoning structure entirely, Catherine developed what she calls "flexible consistency"—maintaining her fasting practice while adapting specific parameters based on life circumstances and body signals.

"The third year brought another evolution," she explains. "Fasting became so integrated into my routine that I rarely tracked specific hours anymore. Instead, I developed more intuitive awareness of when my body felt ready to eat and when I benefited from extending my fast. This wasn't about abandoning structure but rather internalizing it to the point where external tracking became unnecessary."

This progression toward intuitive practice—while maintaining the core benefits that initially attracted her to fasting—allowed Catherine to navigate various life challenges without abandoning her practice. When she changed jobs in her fourth year of fasting, the flexibility she'd developed helped her adapt her approach to new schedule demands rather than seeing the transition as a reason to stop completely.

"What's sustained my practice over five years isn't rigid adherence but rather the tangible benefits I continue experiencing," Catherine reflects. "The weight management that initially motivated me has remained stable, but the mental clarity, simplified relationship with food, and consistent energy have become equally important reasons to continue. When I occasionally take breaks—like during vacations—I notice the difference in how I feel, which naturally motivates returning to my practice."

This evolution of motivation—from external factors like weight to internal experiences like energy and clarity—characterizes many successful long-term practitioners. Rather than requiring constant willpower, their practice becomes self-reinforcing through direct experience of benefits.

Catherine's approach has evolved to include:

1. A typical 16-hour fast most days, but with flexibility based on her monthly cycle
2. Shorter fasts (12-14 hours) during high-stress periods or when sleep quality suffers
3. Occasional longer fasts (20-24 hours) when particularly beneficial or naturally occurring
4. Strategic adjustments for social events without abandoning her practice entirely
5. Minimal formal tracking, replaced by developed body awareness
6. A focus on quality of eating windows rather than just fasting duration
7. Integration with other health practices like movement, stress management, and sleep hygiene

"The key to sustainability hasn't been perfection but integration," Catherine emphasizes. "Fasting has become part of who I am and how I live rather than something separate I'm trying to maintain. The practice has evolved as I've evolved, remaining responsive to my changing needs while continuing to provide its core benefits."

Continuing Journey Checklist: Sustainable Long-Term Practice

Use this checklist to support your evolution from beginner to experienced practitioner:

1. Develop body awareness tools that help you recognize your unique patterns and optimal approach.
2. Create flexible consistency by establishing core practices while allowing appropriate adaptation.
3. Build support systems that normalize and reinforce your continued practice.
4. Periodically reassess benefits to maintain connection with meaningful outcomes beyond initial goals.
5. Cultivate intrinsic motivation focused on how fasting makes you feel rather than external validation.
6. Develop personalized troubleshooting strategies for common challenges in your specific life context.
7. Create environmental supports that make your practice easier to maintain consistently.
8. Establish rhythms of reflection to regularly consider how your practice might evolve with your changing life.

9. Connect with experienced practitioners who can share perspective on long-term integration.
10. Schedule periodic learning updates to stay informed about evolving research and approaches.
11. Practice strategic flexibility during major life transitions rather than all-or-nothing thinking.
12. Integrate fasting with complementary health practices for synergistic wellbeing.
13. Develop clear communication approaches for explaining your practice when relevant.
14. Create celebration rhythms to acknowledge your consistency and evolution.
15. Maintain openness to evolution as your body, circumstances, and understanding change.

The Journey Continues

As we conclude this chapter of questions and answers, remember that your fasting journey represents an ongoing exploration rather than a destination to reach. The questions you have today will evolve into new inquiries as your practice develops, and the challenges you currently face will transform into different opportunities for growth and refinement.

What makes intermittent fasting particularly valuable as a health practice is precisely this evolutionary quality —its ability to grow and adapt with you through different life phases, challenges, and discoveries. The beginner's structured approach gradually evolves into a more intuitive practice that remains responsive to your changing needs while continuing to provide meaningful benefits.

Your path forward will be uniquely yours. Some will find their optimal practice involves consistent daily fasting windows that vary little over time. Others will develop more cyclical approaches that flex with their body's rhythms and life demands. Still others may integrate periodic longer fasts within their regular patterns as their practice matures. The "right" approach is ultimately the one that enhances your wellbeing while integrating sustainably into your life.

As you continue beyond the foundations we've explored in this book, maintain both curiosity about new possibilities and trust in your growing body wisdom. The questions you've learned to ask—How does this feel in my body? What patterns am I noticing? How might I adapt this to my unique needs?—will serve you far beyond specific fasting protocols or schedules.

The journey ahead holds continuing discovery, periodic challenges, and deeper integration. Approach it with patient experimentation rather than rigid expectation, and you'll find that intermittent fasting becomes not just something you do but a valuable lens through which you understand your body's needs, capabilities, and wisdom.

REFERENCES AND BIBLIOGRAPHY

This comprehensive reference section lists all scientific studies, books, articles, and other resources cited throughout the text. Organized alphabetically by author's last name, this section provides complete citation information to support the evidence-based approach of this book and offers resources for further reading and exploration.

A

Aksungar, F. B., Sarıkaya, M., Coskun, A., Serteser, M., & Unsal, I. (2017). Comparison of intermittent fasting versus caloric restriction in obese subjects: A two year follow-up. Journal of Nutrition, Health & Aging, 21(6), 681-688. https://doi.org/10.1007/s12603-016-0786-y

Anton, S. D., Moehl, K., Donahoo, W. T., Marosi, K., Lee, S. A., Mainous, A. G., Leeuwenburgh, C., & Mattson, M. P. (2018). Flipping the metabolic switch: Understanding and applying health benefits of fasting. Obesity, 26(2), 254-268. https://doi.org/10.1002/oby.22065

Antoni, R., Robertson, T. M., Robertson, M. D., & Johnston, J. D. (2018). A pilot feasibility study exploring the effects of a moderate time-restricted feeding intervention on energy intake, adiposity and metabolic physiology in free-living human subjects. Journal of Nutritional Science, 7, e22. https://doi.org/10.1017/jns.2018.13

Antoni, R., Johnston, K. L., Collins, A. L., & Robertson, M. D. (2018). Intermittent v. continuous energy restriction: differential effects on postprandial glucose and lipid metabolism following matched weight loss in overweight/obese participants. British Journal of Nutrition, 119(5), 507-516. https://doi.org/10.1017/S0007114517003890

Ashtary-Larky, D., Bagheri, R., Asbaghi, O., Tinsley, G. M., Kooti, W., Abbasnezhad, A., Afrisham, R., & Wong, A. (2022). Effects of Ramadan intermittent fasting on inflammatory biomarkers and body composition in healthy people: A systematic review and meta-analysis. Nutrients, 14(5), 1028. https://doi.org/10.3390/nu14051028

B

Barnosky, A. R., Hoddy, K. K., Unterman, T. G., & Varady, K. A. (2014). Intermittent fasting vs daily calorie restriction for type 2 diabetes prevention: a review of human findings. Translational Research, 164(4), 302-311. https://doi.org/10.1016/j.trsl.2014.05.013

Bays, J. C. (2017). Mindful eating: A guide to rediscovering a healthy and joyful relationship with food. Shambhala Publications.

Bikman, B. (2020). Why we get sick: The hidden epidemic at the root of most chronic disease—and how to fight it. BenBella Books.

Brown, J. E., Mosley, M., & Aldred, S. (2013). Intermittent fasting: a dietary intervention for prevention of diabetes and cardiovascular disease? British Journal of Diabetes & Vascular Disease, 13(2), 68-72. https://doi.org/10.1177/1474651413486496

C

Carter, S., Clifton, P. M., & Keogh, J. B. (2018). Effect of intermittent compared with continuous energy restricted diet on glycemic control in patients with type 2 diabetes: A randomized noninferiority trial. JAMA Network Open, 1(3), e180756. https://doi.org/10.1001/jamanetworkopen.2018.0756

Chaix, A., Manoogian, E. N. C., Melkani, G. C., & Panda, S. (2019). Time-restricted eating to prevent and manage chronic metabolic diseases. Annual Review of Nutrition, 39, 291-315. https://doi.org/10.1146/annurev-nutr-082018-124320

Choi, I. Y., Piccio, L., Childress, P., Bollman, B., Ghosh, A., Brandhorst, S., Suarez, J., Michalsen, A., Cross, A. H., Morgan, T. E., Wei, M., Paul, F., Bock, M., & Longo, V. D. (2016). A diet mimicking fasting promotes regeneration and reduces autoimmunity and multiple sclerosis symptoms. Cell Reports, 15(10), 2136-2146. https://doi.org/10.1016/j.celrep.2016.05.009

Choi, I. Y., Lee, C., & Longo, V. D. (2017). Nutrition and fasting mimicking diets in the prevention and treatment of autoimmune diseases and immunosenescence. Molecular and Cellular Endocrinology, 455, 4-12. https://doi.org/10.1016/j.mce.2017.01.042

Choi, Y. J., Jeon, S. M., & Shin, S. (2019). Impact of a ketogenic diet on metabolic parameters in patients with obesity or overweight and with or without type 2 diabetes: A meta-analysis of randomized controlled trials. Nutrients, 11(9), 2093. https://doi.org/10.3390/nu11092093

Cienfuegos, S., Gabel, K., Kalam, F., Ezpeleta, M., Wiseman, E., Pavlou, V., Lin, S., Oliveira, M. L., & Varady, K. A. (2020). Effects of 4- and 6-h time-restricted feeding on weight and cardiometabolic health: A randomized controlled trial in adults with obesity. Cell Metabolism, 32(3), 366-378. https://doi.org/10.1016/j.cmet.2020.06.018

D

de Cabo, R., & Mattson, M. P. (2019). Effects of intermittent fasting on health, aging, and disease. New England Journal of Medicine, 381(26), 2541-2551. https://doi.org/10.1056/NEJMra1905136

Di Francesco, A., Di Germanio, C., Bernier, M., & de Cabo, R. (2018). A time to fast. Science, 362(6416), 770-775. https://doi.org/10.1126/science.aau2095

F

Faris, M. A. E., Kacimi, S., Al-Kurd, R. A., Fararjeh, M. A., Bustanji, Y. K., Mohammad, M. K., & Salem, M. L. (2012). Intermittent fasting during Ramadan attenuates proinflammatory cytokines and immune cells in healthy subjects. Nutrition Research, 32(12), 947-955. https://doi.org/10.1016/j.nutres.2012.06.021

Fitzgerald, K. C., Vizthum, D., Henry-Barron, B., Schweitzer, A., Cassard, S. D., Kossoff, E., Hartman, A. L., Kapogiannis, D., Sullivan, P., Baer, D. J., Mattson, M. P., Appel, L. J., & Mowry, E. M. (2018). Effect of intermittent vs. daily calorie restriction on changes in weight and patient-reported outcomes in people with multiple sclerosis. Multiple Sclerosis and Related Disorders, 23, 33-39. https://doi.org/10.1016/j.msard.2018.05.002

Fuhrman, J. (1995). Fasting and eating for health: A medical doctor's program for conquering disease. St. Martin's Press.

Fung, J., & Moore, J. (2016). The complete guide to fasting: Heal your body through intermittent, alternate-day, and extended fasting. Victory Belt Publishing.

Fung, J. (2016). The obesity code: Unlocking the secrets of weight loss. Greystone Books.

G

Gabel, K., Hoddy, K. K., Haggerty, N., Song, J., Kroeger, C. M., Trepanowski, J. F., Panda, S., & Varady, K. A. (2018). Effects of 8-hour time restricted feeding on body weight and metabolic disease risk factors in obese adults: A pilot study. Nutrition and Healthy Aging, 4(4), 345-353. https://doi.org/10.3233/NHA-170036

Golbidi, S., Daiber, A., Korac, B., Li, H., Essop, M. F., & Laher, I. (2017). Health benefits of fasting and caloric restriction. Current Diabetes Reports, 17(12), 123. https://doi.org/10.1007/s11892-017-0951-7

Grajower, M. M., & Horne, B. D. (2019). Clinical management of intermittent fasting in patients with diabetes mellitus. Nutrients, 11(4), 873. https://doi.org/10.3390/nu11040873

Guyenet, S. J. (2017). The hungry brain: Outsmarting the instincts that make us overeat. Flatiron Books.

H

Harvie, M. N., Pegington, M., Mattson, M. P., Frystyk, J., Dillon, B., Evans, G., Cuzick, J., Jebb, S. A., Martin, B., Cutler, R. G., Son, T. G., Maudsley, S., Carlson, O. D., Egan, J. M., Flyvbjerg, A., & Howell, A. (2011). The effects of intermittent or continuous energy restriction on weight loss and metabolic disease risk markers: a randomized trial in young overweight women. International Journal of Obesity, 35(5), 714-727. https://doi.org/10.1038/ijo.2010.171

Harvie, M., & Howell, A. (2017). Potential benefits and harms of intermittent energy restriction and intermittent fasting amongst obese, overweight and normal weight subjects—A narrative review of human and animal evidence. Behavioral Sciences, 7(1), 4. https://doi.org/10.3390/bs7010004

Hutchison, A. T., Regmi, P., Manoogian, E. N. C., Fleischer, J. G., Wittert, G. A., Panda, S., & Heilbronn, L. K. (2019). Time-restricted feeding improves glucose tolerance in men at risk for type 2 diabetes: A randomized crossover trial. Obesity, 27(5), 724-732. https://doi.org/10.1002/oby.22449

J

Jamshed, H., Beyl, R. A., Della Manna, D. L., Yang, E. S., Ravussin, E., & Peterson, C. M. (2019). Early time-restricted feeding improves 24-hour glucose levels and affects markers of the circadian clock, aging, and autophagy in humans. Nutrients, 11(6), 1234. https://doi.org/10.3390/nu11061234

Jordan, S., Tung, N., Casanova-Acebes, M., Chang, C., Cantoni, C., Zhang, D., Wirtz, T. H., Naik, S., Rose, S. A., Brocker, C. N., Gainullina, A., Hornburg, D., Horng, S., Maier, B. B., Cravedi, P., LeRoith, D., Gonzalez, F. J., Meissner, F., Ochando, J., Rahman, A., ... Merad, M. (2019). Voluntary time-restricted feeding reduces chronic inflammation in obesity. Cell Metabolism, 30(1), 92-104. https://doi.org/10.1016/j.cmet.2019.05.010

K

Kalam, F., Gabel, K., Cienfuegos, S., Wiseman, E., Ezpeleta, M., Steward, M., Pavlou, V., & Varady, K. A. (2019). Alternate day fasting combined with a low-carbohydrate diet for weight loss, weight maintenance, and metabolic disease risk reduction. Obesity Science & Practice, 5(6), 531-539. https://doi.org/10.1002/osp4.367

Kaplan, A. (1985). Jewish meditation: A practical guide. Schocken Books.

Kelder, P. (1985). Ancient secret of the fountain of youth. Harbor Press.

L

Longo, V. D., & Mattson, M. P. (2014). Fasting: molecular mechanisms and clinical applications. Cell Metabolism, 19(2), 181-192. https://doi.org/10.1016/j.cmet.2013.12.008

Longo, V. D., & Panda, S. (2016). Fasting, circadian rhythms, and time-restricted feeding in healthy lifespan. Cell Metabolism, 23(6), 1048-1059. https://doi.org/10.1016/j.cmet.2016.06.001

Longo, V. D. (2018). The longevity diet: Discover the new science behind stem cell activation and regeneration to slow aging, fight disease, and optimize weight. Avery.

Lustig, R. H. (2021). Metabolical: The lure and the lies of processed food, nutrition, and modern medicine. Harper Wave.

M

Mattson, M. P., Longo, V. D., & Harvie, M. (2017). Impact of intermittent fasting on health and disease processes. Ageing Research Reviews, 39, 46-58. https://doi.org/10.1016/j.arr.2016.10.005

Mattson, M. P., Moehl, K., Ghena, N., Schmaedick, M., & Cheng, A. (2018). Intermittent metabolic switching, neuroplasticity and brain health. Nature Reviews Neuroscience, 19(2), 63-80. https://doi.org/10.1038/nrn.2017.156

Mindikoglu, A. L., Opekun, A. R., Gagan, S. K., & Devaraj, S. (2020). Impact of time-restricted feeding and dawn-to-sunset fasting on circadian rhythm, obesity, metabolic syndrome, and nonalcoholic fatty liver disease. Gastroenterology Research and Practice, 2020, 3560414. https://doi.org/10.1155/2020/3560414

Minich, D. M. (2020). The science and art of herbalism: Integrating medicinal plants into clinical practice. American Botanical Council.

Minich, D. M. (2020). Circadian nutrition: Using time-restricted eating to improve health and address chronic disease. Metagenics Institute.

Moro, T., Tinsley, G., Bianco, A., Marcolin, G., Pacelli, Q. F., Battaglia, G., Palma, A., Gentil, P., Neri, M., & Paoli, A. (2016). Effects of eight weeks of time-restricted feeding (16/8) on basal metabolism, maximal strength, body composition, inflammation, and cardiovascular risk factors in resistance-trained males. Journal of Translational Medicine, 14(1), 290. https://doi.org/10.1186/s12967-016-1044-0

N

Nhat Hanh, T., & Cheung, L. (2011). Mindful eating, mindful life: Savoring the present moment and the future of your health. HarperOne.

P

Panda, S. (2018). The circadian code: Lose weight, supercharge your energy, and transform your health from morning to midnight. Rodale Books.

Parr, E. B., Devlin, B. L., Radford, B. E., & Hawley, J. A. (2020). A delayed morning and earlier evening time-restricted feeding protocol for improving glycemic control and dietary adherence in men with overweight/obesity: A randomized controlled trial. Nutrients, 12(2), 505. https://doi.org/10.3390/nu12020505

Patterson, R. E., & Sears, D. D. (2017). Metabolic effects of intermittent fasting. Annual Review of Nutrition, 37, 371-393. https://doi.org/10.1146/annurev-nutr-071816-064634

Patterson, R. E., Laughlin, G. A., LaCroix, A. Z., Hartman, S. J., Natarajan, L., Senger, C. M., Martínez, M. E., Villaseñor, A., Sears, D. D., Marinac, C. R., & Gallo, L. C. (2015). Intermittent fasting and human metabolic health. Journal of the Academy of Nutrition and Dietetics, 115(8), 1203-1212. https://doi.org/10.1016/j.jand.2015.02.018

Pelz, M. (2021). The complete guide to fasting for women: A comprehensive guide to intermittent, alternate-day, and extended fasting. Mindful Medicine Publishing.

Phillips, M. C. L., Deprez, D., Owens, A. P., Zatorre, R. J., & Willis, M. K. (2022). Effect of intermittent versus continuous energy restriction on brain health: A randomized controlled trial. Neurology, 99(7), e709-e721. https://doi.org/10.1212/WNL.0000000000200371

R

Rynders, C. A., Thomas, E. A., Zaman, A., Pan, Z., Catenacci, V. A., & Melanson, E. L. (2019). Effectiveness of intermittent fasting and time-restricted feeding compared to continuous energy restriction for weight loss. Nutrients, 11(10), 2442. https://doi.org/10.3390/nu11102442

S

Stekovic, S., Hofer, S. J., Tripolt, N., Aon, M. A., Royer, P., Pein, L., Stadler, J. T., Pendl, T., Prietl, B., Url, J., Schroeder, S., Tadic, J., Eisenberg, T., Magnes, C., Pieber, M., Müller, E., Gasser, L., Kresoja, E., Cardona, S., Chiuve, S. E., ... Madeo, F. (2019). Alternate day fasting improves physiological and molecular markers of aging in healthy, non-obese humans. Cell Metabolism, 30(3), 462-476. https://doi.org/10.1016/j.cmet.2019.07.016

Stephens, G. (2020). Fast. Feast. Repeat.: The comprehensive guide to delay, don't deny intermittent fasting. St. Martin's Griffin.

Sutton, E. F., Beyl, R., Early, K. S., Cefalu, W. T., Ravussin, E., & Peterson, C. M. (2018). Early time-restricted feeding improves insulin sensitivity, blood pressure, and oxidative stress even without weight loss in men with prediabetes. Cell Metabolism, 27(6), 1212-1221.e3. https://doi.org/10.1016/j.cmet.2018.04.010

T

Tello, M., & Gustin, M. B. (2021). The impact of intermittent fasting on metabolism, inflammation, and chronic disease: A narrative review. Journal of Clinical Medicine, 10(5), 1056. https://doi.org/10.3390/jcm10051056

Tinsley, G. M., Moore, M. L., Graybeal, A. J., Paoli, A., Kim, Y., Gonzales, J. U., Harry, J. R., VanDusseldorp, T. A., Kennedy, D. N., & Cruz, M. R. (2019). Time-restricted feeding plus resistance training in active females: a randomized trial. The American Journal of Clinical Nutrition, 110(3), 628-640. https://doi.org/10.1093/ajcn/nqz126

Trepanowski, J. F., Kroeger, C. M., Barnosky, A., Klempel, M. C., Bhutani, S., Hoddy, K. K., Gabel, K., Freels, S., Rigdon, J., Rood, J., Ravussin, E., & Varady, K. A. (2017). Effect of alternate-day fasting on weight loss, weight maintenance, and cardioprotection among metabolically healthy obese adults: A randomized clinical trial. JAMA Internal Medicine, 177(7), 930-938. https://doi.org/10.1001/jamainternmed.2017.0936

V

Varady, K. A., Cienfuegos, S., Ezpeleta, M., & Gabel, K. (2021). Clinical application of intermittent fasting for weight loss: progress and future directions. Nature Reviews Endocrinology, 18(5), 309-321. https://doi.org/10.1038/s41574-022-00638-x

W

Wei, M., Brandhorst, S., Shelehchi, M., Mirzaei, H., Cheng, C. W., Budniak, J., Groshen, S., Mack, W. J., Guen, E., Di Biase, S., Cohen, P., Morgan, T. E., Dorff, T., Hong, K., Michalsen, A., Laviano, A., & Longo, V. D. (2017). Fasting-mimicking diet and markers/risk factors for aging, diabetes, cancer, and cardiovascular disease. Science Translational Medicine, 9(377), eaai8700. https://doi.org/10.1126/scitranslmed.aai8700

Welton, S., Minty, R., O'Driscoll, T., Willms, H., Poirier, D., Madden, S., & Kelly, L. (2020). Intermittent fasting and weight loss: Systematic review. Canadian Family

Physician, 66(2), 117-125.

Wilkinson, M. J., Manoogian, E. N. C., Zadourian, A., Lo, H., Fakhouri, S., Shoghi, A., Wang, X., Fleischer, J. G., Navlakha, S., Panda, S., & Taub, P. R. (2020). Ten-hour time-restricted eating reduces weight, blood pressure, and atherogenic lipids in patients with metabolic syndrome. Cell Metabolism, 31(1), 92-104.e5. https://doi.org/10.1016/j.cmet.2019.11.004

Witte, A. V., Fobker, M., Gellner, R., Knecht, S., & Flöel, A. (2009). Caloric restriction improves memory in elderly humans. Proceedings of the National Academy of Sciences, 106(4), 1255-1260. https://doi.org/10.1073/pnas.0808587106

Printed in Dunstable, United Kingdom

64701712R00198